PRAISE FOR THIS BOOK

"Kaufman and Guerra-López have written the ultimate needs assessment text. A practical guide that's fully comprehensive, full of tools, yet written in a style easily understood by anyone undertaking such a task for any institution."

Steven J. Kelly

Partner, KNO Worldwide

"Kaufman and Guerra-López offer exceptional guidance for any organization seeking long-term success. Their comprehensive focus on the process of designing and implementing organizational strategy from Mega to Micro elements is clearly and effectively presented. Any organization or enterprise will benefit greatly from following the guidance provided by these experienced, world-class scholars."

John V. Lombardi

President Emeritus, University of Florida

"*Needs Assessment for Organizational Success* is a guide book for pragmatic professionals who want to know how to achieve desired goals, while also containing sound philosophical bases for those who want to understand the principles underlying successful goal-setting and organizational guidance. Written by two world-class experts, this book provides the reader with an invaluable insight into organizational direction and success."

Caesar Naples

Vice Chancellor Emeritus, The California State University

"This book is an excellent and comprehensive development of the life work of Roger Kaufman, arguably the father of modern needs assessment. The text lays out his fundamental methodology for needs assessment, namely defining a 'need' as a noun and showing how to quantify the gap between actual and desired results. It integrates Kaufman's notable contribution, the Organizational Elements Model, which introduced the concept of a Mega level that explicitly incorporated a link to societal good in strategic planning. The authors provide a plethora of tools for those who wish to implement these ideas to seek organizational success."

William Swart, PhD

Professor of Marketing and Supply Chain Management, East Carolina University

i

"Finally, a needs assessment book that connects to organizational success. Moving beyond typical learning needs assessment, this new book focuses on four levels of needs, a shift that's required in today's environment. Written in an easy-to-read format with practical tools, this is a must-have reference for learning and performance improvement professionals."

Jack J. Phillips, PhD

Chairman, ROI Institute

"Kaufman and Guerra-López take us into the world of needs assessment in their new book, *Needs Assessment for Organizational Success*. They give us the tools and resources required to look at organizations across five elements: Mega (societal), Macro (organizational), Micro (individual), Processes, and Inputs; and their evidence-based approach can be used in both public and private sectors. For clear and practical techniques, add this book to your performance improvement library."

Dr. Roger M. Addison, CPT

Chief Performance Officer, Addison Consulting

"*Needs Assessment for Organizational Success* is the new and central tool for organizations determined to be the organization of the future. Levels of needs assessment move us toward a new level of understanding of the bright future we all desire."

Frances Hesselbein

President & CEO, The Frances Hesselbein Leadership Institute

Founding President, The Drucker Foundation

Former CEO, The Girl Scouts of the USA

"My work in large and small organizations with the constructs and methods of Roger Kaufman goes back more than 20 years. This latest book with Ingrid Guerra-López continues and builds on the path finding Mega planning. The new book is pragmatic, practical, and sensible. It is a blueprint for any organization that seeks to add value to all stakeholders and then be able to prove it."

Peter Sharp

Company Director, Canberra Australia

"Successful managers know that front-end analysis of needs and gaps is a necessary component of organizational success. Yet impulsive, over-confident decision making has been found to be one of the major barriers to organizational success. This book provides the reader with careful, smart, and efficient evidence-based approaches to needs assessment. Roger Kaufman and Ingrid Guerra-Lopez have been thought leaders in this area for many years and this book distills the learning of many different kinds of organizations about a number of needs analysis methods."

Dr. Richard Clark

Professor of Educational Psychology and Technology, Rossier School of Education
Professor of Clinical Research in Surgery, Keck School of Medicine
University of Southern California

"Kaufman and Guerra-López provide a simple statement of the Mega Planning Model by pulling together Quasi needs assessment, while the vital signs for the organization make it easy to connect and allow flexibility. They also provide improved tools and approaches that fill out the many requirements of the planning process, while neatly separating the assessor, 'what can we expect?' from the evaluator, 'what did we get?' Mega Planning asks us to create something of truly lasting value with everything we undertake."

Dr. Ronald Forbes

Leaderskill Group Pty Ltd

"The authors provide proven evidence-based concepts, methods, and tools for measurably improving organizational success, in both the public and private sectors. It works, and works well."

Dominic M. Calabro

President & CEO, Florida TaxWatch

NEEDS

Roger Kaufman + Ingrid Guerra-López

ASSESSMENT

for Organizational Success

ASTD
WORKPLACE LEARNING & PERFORMANCE
PRESS

22 21 20 19 18   3 4 5 6 7

ASTD Press is an internationally renowned source of insightful and practical information on workplace learning, performance, and professional development.

ASTD Press
1640 King Street Box 1443
Alexandria, VA 22313-1443 USA

Ordering information: Books published by ASTD Press can be purchased by visiting ASTD's website at store.astd.org or by calling 800.628.2783 or 703.683.8100.

Library of Congress Control Number: 2012940626

ISBN-10: 1-56286-814-4
ISNB-13: 978-1-56286-814-7
e-ISBN: 978-1-60728-736-0

ASTD Press Editorial Staff:
Director: Glenn Saltzman
Manager, ASTD Press: Ashley McDonald
Community of Practice Manager, Learning and Development: Juana Llorens
Editorial Assistant: Sarah Cough
Text and Cover Design: Lon Levy

Printed by Data Reproductions Corporation, Auburn Hills, MI

Table of Contents

Preface

Successful needs assessment is all about the choices you make. Choose wisely, and success is all but certain. Make another choice and failure is guaranteed.

While this book will be a valuable resource for anyone interested in an evidence-based approach to improve organizational performance, it is written specifically for performance improvement professionals (including workplace learning and development professionals) who want to make good decisions that lead to productive results.

These internal and external organizational players and stakeholders are individuals involved in organizational planning and include those who manage or administer any needs assessment, change, evaluation, or any other related initiatives intended to improve organizational performance.

The book will also be a valuable resource for those who support, manage, or make direct decisions about an organization's overall strategic direction, including executives, administrators, members of a company's leadership team, or even external performance consulting professionals.

Primary Focus on Strategic Alignment

The intended audience and scope of this book is broad; it purposefully does not deal with the full range of specific data collection methodology or approaches since many good resources already exist on this topic. Rather, this book focuses on the job of building a properly aligned needs assessment framework that will ensure you:

- make the right long-, short,- and mid-term needs assessment choices

- are heading in the right direction

- arrive at your intended destination

- properly align results at various organizational levels

- identify real problems (such as gaps in results), not just symptoms

- develop valid and reliable criteria for selecting the most effective and efficient solutions and interventions

- link everything done, produced, or delivered (both inside and out) by your organization

- fully track performance gaps (from needs assessment through evaluation) using well-designed and implemented performance dashboards.

Four Levels of Needs Assessment

In addition to its singular focus on building an effective needs assessment framework, this book offers a unique, four-level system to categorize needs assessment efforts: Mega, Macro, Micro, and Quasi. These various levels are outlined below:

- *Mega Needs Assessment:* A strategic needs assessment that incorporates a systemic perspective of the organization, society, and their gaps in results.

- *Macro Needs Assessment:* A tactical needs assessment that begins with a primary focus on organizational gaps in results, independent of its external/societal context.

- *Micro Needs Assessment:* An operational needs assessment that focuses primarily on internal performance gaps of individuals, teams, or departments within an organization.

- *Quasi Needs Assessment:* In contrast to the previously mentioned needs assessment, this level does not focus on performance results. Rather this needs assessment focuses on identifying gaps in means (for example training or other solutions). Training needs assessment is an example of a Quasi needs assessment.

Making the Most of This Book

While the book is constructed to allow you to pick and choose which chapters or sections are most applicable or useful to your particular needs, it is strongly recommended that you read all the chapters to gain full understanding and value from the book. Still, if you wish to take a piecemeal approach, then use the job aid on the following page to determine the chapters that will be most useful to you.

Other Reader Notes

Recurring Case Study

Beginning in chapter 3 we offer a recurring narrative using a fictional organization, Bewell Insurance Company (BIC), intended to illustrate the concepts discussed in this book. In this narrative BIC is facing an important change with new legislation that mandates health insurance for all United States citizens. This will have an impact at all levels of the organization; in particular, the chief operating officer has asked to help the executive team figure out how to maintain BIC's leadership in the industry, especially in terms of profitability.

Readers in other industries (for example, education, military, nonprofit) will also find relevant performance issues in this case study, and are encouraged to read through the case study carefully.

If you are:	Then read:
Interested in understanding the performance improvement process and how needs assessment supports continuous performance improvement	All chapters
Interested in learning about foundational concepts in performance driven needs assessments	Chapter 1: Needs Assessment and Performance Improvement Chapter 2: Basic Tools for a Useful Assessment
Concerned with identifying strategic needs that takes into account external environmental (for example, societal) factors and consequences	Chapter 3: Performing a Mega-Level Needs Assessment
Concerned with identifying tactical needs that take into account the entire organization	Chapter 4: Performing a Macro-Level Needs Assessment
Concerned with identifying operational needs that take into account only individuals, teams, and other subsystems of the organization	Chapter 5: Performing a Micro-Level Needs Assessment
Concerned with identifying gaps that relate to specific solutions, such as training	Chapter 6: Performing a Quasi Needs Assessment
Interested in maximizing solution alternatives and assuring selected solutions address root causes of gaps, rather than only symptoms	Chapter 7: Linking Analysis and Solutions to Make Recommendations
Interested in continual improvement by linking needs assessment and evaluation	Chapter 8: Linking Needs Assessment to Evaluation
Interested in how to keep track of trends in performance gaps, and what contributes to their reduction versus maintenance	Chapter 9: Performance Dashboards: Monitoring Performance Gaps
Interested in questionnaires as one of many data collection tools used for needs assessment	Chapter 10: Gap Assessment Tools
Interested in exercises that will help you and your stakeholders enter into useful dialog and actions related to needs assessment, particularly at the Mega level	Chapter 11: Tool Kit

Chapter by Chapter Notes

Below is an outline of the primary topics covered in each chapter.

- **Chapter 1—Needs Assessment and Performance Improvement:** Foundational concepts in performance driven needs assessments.

- **Chapter 2—Basic Tools for a Useful Assessment:** Using the Organizational Elements Model as a needs assessment framework.

- **Chapter 3—Performing a Mega-Level Needs Assessment:** Describes the process for conducting a Mega-level needs assessment and other important considerations.

- **Chapter 4—Performing a Macro-Level Needs Assessment:** Describes the process for conducting a Macro-level needs assessment and other important considerations.

- **Chapter 5—Performing a Micro-Level Needs Assessment:** Describes the process for conducting a Micro-level needs assessment and other important considerations.

- **Chapter 6—Performing a Quasi Needs Assessment**: Describes the process for conducting a Quasi-level needs assessment and other important considerations.

- **Chapter 7—Linking Analysis and Solutions to Make Recommendations:** Describes how to link needs assessment, analysis, and recommendations, providing various analysis tools.

- **Chapter 8—Linking Needs Assessment to Evaluation:** Describes how to link needs assessment and evaluation for continuous improvement.

- **Chapter 9—Performance Dashboards: Monitoring Performance Gaps:** Describes key uses in the design, implementation and use of performance dashboards, and the data that emerge from them.

- **Chapter 10—Gap Assessment Tools:** Provides examples of specific data collection tools focused on gaps, and discusses ways to use these tools, as well as how to interpret and use findings.

- **Chapter 11—Tool Kit:** Provides a series of practical tools for use in meetings, presentations, and various communications with needs assessment and planning stakeholders.

This book is about success: yours, your associates', your organization's, and how those contribute to a better society. It is pragmatic, sensible, and useful.

Acknowledgments

Thank you for reading this book and applying it to improve our world through the success of your organization. It is shared in a spirit of personal, organizational, and societal growth.

We wish to thank many people, too numerous to mention all, including our families, colleagues, students, and clients. Each and all have educated us and will continue to do so.

We want to thank ASTD for helping us bring this book to reality, especially Tony Bingham and our editors, Juana Llorens and Ashley McDonald; and also, the entire ASTD team, who take our profession seriously enough to make evidence-based concepts and tools available.

Roger Kaufman
Tallahassee, Florida

Ingrid Guerra-López
Detroit, Michigan

Chapter 1
Needs Assessment
and Performance Improvement

What's in This Chapter?

- How to clearly justify your organization's direction

- Understanding your assessment choices and how to relate means and ends

- Defining "needs" as a gap in results, not a methods, means, or resource discrepancy

- The relationship between needs assessment and evaluation

- How to ensure stakeholder participation and buy-in

Finding Your Way

It is important to make certain that you and your organization are headed in the right direction; this means that you have justified exactly where you are headed and you know how to tell when you have arrived. Finding the right direction is absolutely vital. This chapter provides the basic concepts and tools to assure that when you do needs assessment, you have valid and reliable data upon which to make, and justify, decisions.

The precise definition of words and concepts are absolutely vital, and even if some words sound familiar, we provide unique definitions for many. It is more than semantics and being precise is central to your success.

Introduction: Setting the Right Destination

Most journeys we take are considered successful if we arrive at the right place, at the right time, and in good condition. The "right place" is vital. Identifying where you should head and justifying why you should get there will provide you with the critical data upon which to do planning, design, development, implementation, and monitoring and evaluation. Likewise, performance is not merely about what we do or how we do it, it is first and foremost about accomplishments (or "arriving" at a desired and appropriate destination).

When we talk about improving performance, we are talking about improving our accomplishments, the results of what we do and how we do it. It does us little good to improve what we do and how we do it, if it doesn't improve the results we want to accomplish. First, we define the results we want to accomplish; and then we consider what we should do and how, in order to accomplish them. And that is where needs assessment comes in. It provides concrete data on where you should head, why you should go there, and how to tell when you have arrived. Here are some journey tips and thoughts to consider.

Avoid flaws in conventional thinking and models. If there is a universal mistake in how organizations decide how to improve their effectiveness and efficiency, it's that they tend to start development without a proper review to:

- Ensure that their objectives (including visions and missions) are still appropriate and have enough specificity so that people can appropriately plan to meet them.

- Provide rigorous and clear criteria for management, development, evaluation, and continual improvement. Conventional practice for organizational improvement denies itself the data about where the organization should be going, how to know when it is having success, and how to manage improvement in the organization.

An analogy might be if an airliner left its home airport with no better guidance than "to have a good trip to San Diego," without a practical, tangible, and agreed upon navigation plan for getting there. Conventional practice values quick action under the guise of decisiveness, and often, quick action leads to costly mistakes. Quick action in and of itself is not a bad thing, if it doesn't entail picking solutions before understanding problems and opportunities.

Start with a needs assessment to provide the data for front-end alignment to ensure you're going to the right place. The first action proposed in this book is a pragmatic needs assessment. The approach in this book will remedy the problems lurking in current approaches by focusing on useful ends defined in measurable performance terms. If someone didn't challenge the status quo in measurable terms, we would still be living on a flat earth. This book defers approaches, methods, means, activities, and tools until all organizational effectiveness and improvement partners can measurably articulate, justify, and communicate where to head and why go there. This approach avoids "solutions in search of problems" and starting out a journey with vague notions of where to head (for example, "be world class," "excellence," "delighted customers," "become number one").

A serious organization measurably determines where it is and should be headed, and then concerns itself with arriving on time and in good condition. Then it decides on how to get there. All three are important, but first and foremost we define "where to head."

The sensible road map for a successful journey—for measurably improving what your organization contributes—is based on the general performance improvement process: Assessment, Analysis, Design, Development, Implementation, and Evaluation (AADDIE) (Guerra, 2003), depicted in Figure 1.1. This is a more responsive framework than the conventional ADDIE framework because it doesn't assume that one knows what to analyze, but first assesses where one should head.

The major emphasis of this book is on needs assessment, causal and other types of analyses, as well as the ongoing linkage from needs assessment to evaluation and continual improvement.

Choosing the proper destination for organizational improvement and organizational effectiveness involves change, choices, and consequences (Kaufman, 2006). Change is inevitable and it is a matter of whether you become the master of change or the victim of it. This leads to choices: Do you choose to create a new and better future or just react to it? And then there are consequences of your choices about the change. Do you measurably add value to your organization or do you subtract value?

The choices are yours and your organization's to make and the consequences are yours to realize. Hesitant to make choices? Not making a decision is a decision (Greenwald, 1973). When facing uncertainty, which seems to always be with us, management expert Peter Drucker advises us, "If you can't predict the future, create it." This approach to needs assessment will allow you to define and create the better future for you and your organization. And that means tangibly defining and delivering success; success that you can prove.

Defining and arriving at the right place (at the right time and in the right condition) is facilitated by needs assessments. We'll define what that is and then tell you about the underlying concepts and tools that can help you deliver organizational improvement and success.

Figure 1.1   AADDIE Model

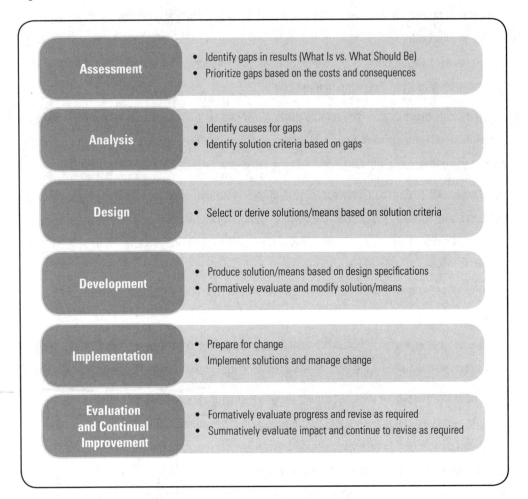

Ends vs. Means

Measurable performance improvement starts with identifying the ends we want to accomplish (not the means we prefer) and then determining our current position with regards to those ends. The distinction between ends and means cannot be overstated.

- **Ends** are results, impacts, and consequences. They are what happens after we use and do something.

- **Means** are the ways we achieve ends. They are the how-to-do it.

Both are important, related, and different. Ends define where we should finish and the means (the right means) get us there. Figure 1.2 further defines these two important elements.

Figure 1.2   Differentiating Ends vs. Means

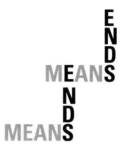

What's the Difference?

ENDS   are the results, impacts, or accomplishments we get from applying the means. They are what is achieved.

MEANS   are the way in which we do something. They are processes, activities, resources, methods or techniques we use to deliver a result.

Source: Kaufman, R. (2011). *The Manager's Pocket Guide to Mega Thinking and Planning.* Amherst, MA: HRD Press.

What Is a Need?

If we are going to assess needs, and use them to set our direction and planning to achieve organizational success, let's define some terms. First, let's define: What is a *need*? A *need* is a gap between current results (and consequences) and desired results and consequences.

Figure 1.3 illustrates this definition of a need as a gap between current and desired results and the consequences of that gap.

The Inherent Conflict of Language

Ordinary language usage provides a challenge for conducting a useful needs assessment. Common usage of "need" often takes us to solutions—we *need* more money, we *need* more time, we *need* more people, we *need* to outsource, we *need* to reorganize—and this always leads us to selecting and applying solutions (more time, more money, etc.) before we know the problem and before we know what results we should deliver. Thus, without thinking, people unknowingly jump into solutions before defining and justifying a problem (a *problem* is a need—a gap in results—chosen for reduction or elimination). This book has an emphasis on results and relevant evidence. The quick way for you to be successful at needs assessment—and maintain a strategic focus—is to act on the realization that **need is a noun: a gap between current results and desired results. It is not a verb.**

Figure 1.3   Definition of Need

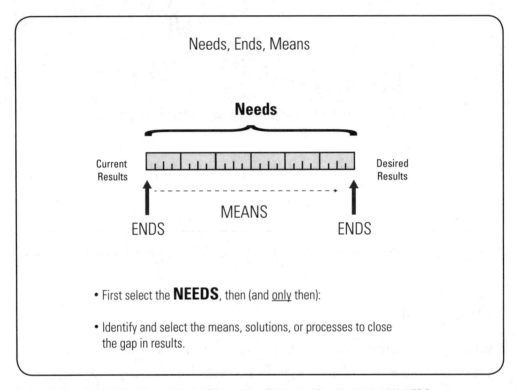

Source: Kaufman, R. (2011). *The Manager's Pocket Guide to Mega Thinking and Planning*. Amherst, MA: HRD Press.

If we use *need* as a noun, we will be able to justify both useful objectives as well as what we do and deliver. We will be able to provide valid rationale and evidence for everything we use, do, produce, and deliver. It is the only sensible way we can demonstrate value added.

By jumping into a solution (a means, methods, intervention, technique, or tool) through the use of *need* as a verb, disagreements often begin about what people want, rather than focusing stakeholders on what must be accomplished. We can argue almost endlessly about which means is better—training, Six Sigma, benchmarking, technology—if we don't define which gap in results a favored means will close. To reduce conflict and the practice of selecting solutions in search of problems, go back to basics: First define the needs (as gaps in results) and then consider and select the means to close those gaps in results.

The Need Word

Need is an overused word. Just listen to everyday conversation, including perhaps yours. And the way the word is used conventionally in needs assessment often leads one to means before defining and justifying the ends to be accomplished. People confuse needs and wants (ends and means) all the time. And the consequences of getting these confused are not pretty. Ever hear a family member say things like:

I need a new car.

I need more time.

I need him/her.

I need more technology.

I need more people.

I need a new dress/suit.

I need to go to the mall.

I need more money.

The difference between ends and means is clear, but it becomes blurred when we use need as a verb. When you use need as a verb, it is very demanding and takes away your choices. There are no longer options, just the solution (more money, more training, more benchmarking, new technology) that have been pre-selected. Thus, people are constantly picking solutions before they know the problems.

Now that we have a definition of *need*—a gap in results—we have the basis for starting to determine the objectives for our organization; for everything we use, do, produce, and deliver in terms of adding value outside our organization; for defining and justifying the right place for us to head and arrive. The tool for this is *needs assessment*.

What Is a Needs Assessment?

A *needs assessment* identifies gaps between current and desired results—not means—and places those in priority order on the basis of the costs to meet the needs as compared to the costs to ignore the needs. These gaps are called needs, and needs chosen for resolution can also be referred to as *problems*. By defining need as the gap between current and required results, we have the basis for justifying not only where we should head but also the evidence for proving the costs of meeting the need—getting to the 'right' destination—as well as the costs for ignoring the need. We have to operate in an environment of trust, and trust is best built through objective evidence.

Defining need as a gap in results provides a triple bonus:

- You determine "what should be," which is derived on the basis of performance data; this becomes your objectives.

- You have the basic criteria for evaluation; you only have to compare the new distance between *What Is* and *What Should Be* based on the needs identified and justified.

- You have the basis for unimpeachable proposals because you can provide both the conventional "cost to meet the need" with the "costs to ignore the need."

Taking this approach has an additional organizational political benefit. If you provide such data in a proposal and it is turned down by the person making the project decision, then any responsibility for failure and the consequences shifts away from you.

Needs Are Not Wants, and Means Are Not Ends

It is critical to understand that there is a wide range of perceptions about what is called a need or a needs assessment. In fact, many so-called needs are not needs at all, but preferred wants. Likewise, many so-called needs assessments are not needs assessments, but rather a survey of wants. For example, picking training as a solution, and then asking your employees to come up with 10 reasons why they *need* training or in what areas they would like training is not a needs assessment. This is an example of how to justify preferred solutions through incomplete data (in this case, popular wants) without first collecting evidence about real gaps, actual causal factors, and a range of relevant options.

Needs Assessment vs. Needs (or Performance) Analysis

Variations of this process have also been referred to as performance analysis (International Society for Performance Improvement, 2011; Pershing, 2006), or assumed to be part of a front-end analysis (Harless, 1975), or a figuring things out (FTO) study (Zemke and Kramlinger, 1982).

However, we caution about blurring assessment with analysis, as one seeks to identify gaps in results, while the other seeks to understand the root causes and essential elements of such gaps. If we refer to a basic *Webster's* definition of analysis, we find that analysis is described as the process of studying the nature of something or determining its essential features and their relations. In this sense, both needs assessment and needs analysis are part of an essential and preliminary stage in any learning and performance improvement effort.

Needs assessment provides data about gaps in results, and therefore sets up the evaluation framework to be used when evaluating the solutions that were implemented to close such gaps (Guerra-López, 2008). Needs analysis should come after a needs assessment in order to provide data about the causal factors of the gaps, and therefore critical input about what solution alternatives should be considered to close such gaps. Indeed analysis is an important and supporting aspect of evaluation—and all performance improvement phases—as one should always seek to better understand gaps between What Is and What Should Be (or what was intended).

Training Needs Assessment Caveat

It is also worth noting the distinction between a performance-based needs assessment and a training needs assessment. The purpose of a training needs assessment is to identify "the things we must know before we train…." (Rossett, 1987, p. 14), which suggests we already know training is the solution to the performance problem. From a performance perspective, needs assessments can be conducted at various levels of organizational results, including strategic (external impact), tactical (overall organizational results), and operational (internal deliverables), independently of any pre-imposed solution(s).

Within an instructional context, needs assessments could be conducted at the learner level, either looking at gaps in knowledge, or preferably, looking at gaps in human performance and behaviors first, and then seeking to identify the relevant gaps in knowledge so as to better target desired results. This is echoed by Dick, Carey, and Carey (2009), who suggest that needs assessment, in the context of instructional design, begins by asking what learners must be able to do or perform, rather than what they must know (Guerra-López in Richey, 2012).

It is also worth noting that although sometimes the terms *needs assessments* and *evaluations* are used interchangeably, they are quite different.

Needs Assessment and Evaluation— Related but Different

While assessors and evaluators may share data collection techniques, the types of questions they seek to answer differ. In this sense, the roles of assessor and evaluator differ in purpose or function, rather than importance and methods. *Needs assessors* help define, justify, and create the future by providing hard and soft data for the identification of performance-based vision, aligned missions, and building-block objectives, as well as the gaps between current and desired results. Additionally, they help identify the best solutions for closing these gaps, and thereby ultimately reaching the organizational vision.

On the other hand, *evaluators* help to determine whether we did in fact reach the future we set out to create during the needs assessment process. One of the primary ways they do this is by determining the effectiveness and efficiency of the implemented programs and solutions, as well as the causal factors associated with any gaps between expected and accomplished results. Measurably improving organizational and individual performance depends heavily on these two roles and processes.

While both assessors and evaluators collect data with regards to the current results of process or activity, evaluators collect data to determine whether current results match the results expected from solutions (such as new programs, new technologies, new processes, training, or any other means we select to help us achieve our objectives) that have already been implemented. The assessor, in contrast, seeks to anticipate the expected return-on-investment of potential interventions before they are implemented by collecting data both about current results (What Is) as well as the potential results (What Should Be). With this data, decision makers are able choose among competing alternatives (Guerra-López, 2008).

Stakeholder Participation and Buy-In

Any successful organizational improvement effort is dependent on the involvement and buy-in of its organizational partners. Needs assessment is no different. You will want to include representatives of all relevant stakeholder groups in your needs assessment. If the very same people charged with defining and accomplishing the results that the organization commits to deliver are not part of the process, they will doubtfully be a willing partner after the fact. Moreover, the needs assessment findings and recommendations will likely be met with skepticism and resentment, which only leads to failed improvement efforts.

While not every stakeholder has to be physically present in needs assessment activities, it is critical that they feel their interests are well represented and considered in the process. A comprehensive and representative stakeholder group should be identified for revisions, feedback, and approval. A subset of this group should form a more active core work group that will collaborate closely with those needs assessors.

As you read through each of the needs assessment levels, keep in mind that all efforts are to be carried out as a needs assessment and planning team.

Needs assessment ensures that you are headed in the right direction, provides the criteria for designing and delivering success, and provides the criteria for determining if you were successful.

Chapter Summary

Organizational improvement and organizational success relies on defining and justifying where we are headed and how to know when we arrive. Needs are gaps in results, not in processes, methods, or means. Needs assessments identify the gaps between *current* results and their consequences and *desired* results and their consequences. They also will provide important data so we can identify the costs of meeting the needs as compared to the costs to ignore them. Needs assessments are not the same thing as needs analysis, performance analysis, or evaluation. In the next chapter we will introduce the basic tools you require to begin your needs assessment.

Chapter 2
Basic Tools for a Useful Needs Assessment

What's in This Chapter?

- A detailed description of the Organizational Elements Model (OEM): a template for planning, design, development, and success

- The most common missing ingredient from a needs assessment (societal value added)

- How to align internal and external results and consequences

The Organizational Elements Model (OEM)

Every organization, whether or not it recognizes it, is a means to societal ends. As performance improvement expert Dale Brethower cautions us, *If you are not adding value to society, you are probably subtracting value.*

Organizational success depends on adding value to all internal stakeholders and those external to the organization. This is vital, and the missing variable on most approaches to needs assessment and indeed strategic planning (Davis, 2005). Every organization, if it intends to survive and thrive, has to add value to its external clients, including society. It is not only good business, but ethical as well (Moore, 2010). No sensible organization wants to hurt, harm, disable, or kill their clients—neglected, irritated, hurt, or dead people are not usually repeat customers. One thing that can make an organization go out of business, lose market share, or damage its public image is to harm its clients, and most organizations care very much about safety. Many years ago, Ford Motor Company lost major market share when it was reported that the Pinto (1971–1980), one of its most popular models, had a major death rate from some crashes.[1] In 1982, on

---

1. http://money.cnn.com/galleries/2007/autos/0708/gallery.questionable_cars/3.html

the other hand, Johnson & Johnson immediately recalled all packages of Tylenol when a tainted package was discovered in Seattle. They replaced it in a tamper-proof form and regained and even added to market share. Social responsibility paid off.[2] Increasing emphasis worldwide is now on environmentally sustainable products and earth-friendly materials. Safety is increasingly a central concern.

The Organizational Elements Model (OEM) provides guidance and direction for serious performance improvement. It has five levels, three related to ends and two to means. Figure 2.1 illustrates the results chain for needs and its alignment to means. A needs assessment is best done at each organizational results level: Mega, Macro, and Micro.

Figure 2.1   Results Chain of the OEM

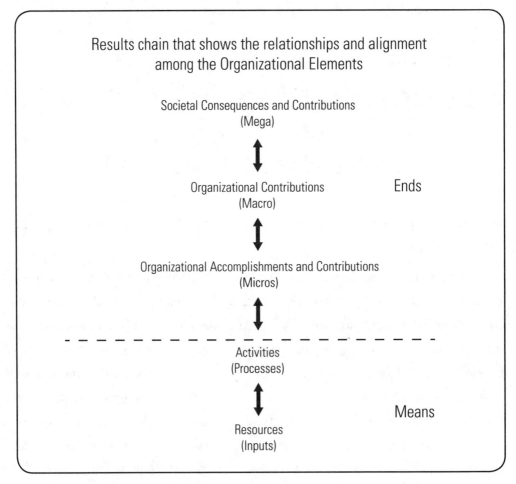

Source: Kaufman, R. (2011). *The Manager's Pocket Guide to Mega Thinking and Planning*. Amherst, MA: HRD Press.

2. http://www.brainmass.com/homework-help/business/marketing/255690

The Five Organizational Elements

The five organizational elements—Mega, Macro, Micro, Processes, and Inputs—must be defined with rigor and precision, and they must also relate one to the others so whatever you use, do, produce, and deliver will add value to our external clients and society. This primary (but not exclusive) attention to Mega—societal value added—is vital, critical, and missing from most other approaches to needs assessment and planning.

The Organizational Elements must be linked and aligned if we are to deliver organizational improvement and success. Doing so enables you to ensure that everything you use (Inputs) and do (Processes) as well as individual results (Micro) and organizational contributions (Outputs) deliver useful societal results (Mega); all in the value chain are both served well and well served. Table 2.1 shows how the organizational elements link and align.

Table 2.1   How the OEM Links to Needs Assessment and Key Stakeholders at Each Level

Organizational Element	Examples	Needs Assessment Level	Type of Planning	Key Stakeholder
Outcomes: Societal results and consequences	Quality of life, health, self-sufficiency, gainfully employed graduates	Mega	Strategic planning	Clients, client's clients, community, society
Outputs: Organizational results	Profits, sales, patients discharged, graduates	Macro	Tactical planning	Organization itself
Products: En-route results or building blocks note there may be multiple levels of products)	Competent employees, courses completed, assembled vehicles, medical procedures completed, accomplished/met standards	Micro	Operational planning	Individual and groups of employees or performers
Processes: Interventions, solutions, methods	Teaching, training, learning, manufacturing, selling, managing, marketing	Quasi	Action planning	Individual and groups of employees or performers
Inputs: Resources	Funding, employees, equipment, regulations, standards	Quasi	Resource planning	Individual and groups of employees or performers

The OEM also provides a framework for critical questions to answer about our needs assessment and indeed all planning, management, implementation, and evaluation. Below are the questions every organization must ask and answer, and the level of planning and name of the type of result (Kaufman, 1998).

Finding Useful Direction and Purposes

- Do you commit to deliver organizational contributions that add measurable value to both your external clients and society? (Mega/Outcomes)

- Do you commit to deliver organizational contributions that have the quality required by your external clients? (Macro/Outputs)

- Do you commit to deliver internal results that have the quality required by your internal partners? (Micro/Products)

- Do you commit to have efficient internal process, programs, projects, and activities? (Processes)

- Do you commit to ensure and deliver the quality and appropriateness of the human, capital, and physical resources required? (Inputs)

These are the important questions that will allow you to align everything you use, do, produce, and deliver to add measurable value within and outside of your organization. Each organizational element is dependent on all others. If one systematically and rigorously answers each of the questions, the chances of success are dramatically increased. If any one element is omitted or not defined rigorously and measurably (see chapter 1) then the operations get sloppy and success is not likely.

Some additional examples for each element are illustrated in Table 2.2.

Why the OEM Is Important to Organizations

When organizations do not align each of the organizational elements, it renders their approach incomplete. It is vital for any useful needs assessment to identify the relevant gaps between What Is and What Should Be for each of the results-referenced organizational elements:

- Mega/Outcomes
- Macro/Outputs
- Micro/Products

Table 2.2   Additional Examples for Each of the Organizational Elements

Mega	• All persons are self-sufficient and self-reliant—not under the care, custody, or control of another person, agency, or substance including the health and well-being • Organizations (including clients and customers) are successful over time including ROI for investors, increased stock value over time* • Eliminated disabling illness due to environmental pollution • Eliminated disabling fatalities • Positive quality of life • No welfare recipients (and thus their consumption is less than their production) • Zero disabling crime • Continued profit over time (5 years and beyond) • Created jobs that add value over time • School completer is self-sufficient and self-reliant
Macro	• Revenue • Profit • Sales • Patient discharged • Graduate • Brand recognition • Intellectual capital outputs (e.g. patents, licenses, etc.) • Total market value added to the organization
Micro	• Production quota met • Competent personnel (as a result of training, for example) • Course successfully completed • Operation completed • Test or course passed
Processes	• Organizational development • Management techniques • Operating production line • 360 feedback • Training • Six Sigma • Examining patient • Strategic (or tactical or operational) planning • Assessing needs • Course development • Budgeting • Communication practices • Use of interpersonal skills
Inputs	• Money • People • Equipment • Facilities • Existing goals • Existing policies • Time • Resources • Individual values • Laws • Current economic conditions • Curriculum • Regulations • History • Organizational culture • Current problems • Existing materials • Current staff and their skills, knowledges, attitudes, and abilities • Characteristics of current and potential clients • Predicted client desires and requirements

*Note: The words "over time" are critical. Success over time indicates that what it delivers to external clients is safe and useful and that is also reflected in continuing profits and no successful liability lawsuits against them.

Consequences of Micro-Only Focus

Suppose you focus only on a commitment to:

- deliver internal results that have the quality required by your internal partners (Micro/Products)

- have efficient internal process, programs, projects, and activities (Processes)

- ensure and deliver the quality and appropriateness of the human, capital, and physical resources required (Inputs).

By following this path your assumption is that whatever Products (for example, mastery of a skill as a result of training, development of a widget, completion of a task) delivered as a result will lead to organizational success. That is a big and dangerous assumption. For example, research shows us that less than 10 percent of what is learned in training transfers to the job (Clark and Estes, 2002).

One should ask: "If I get results at this Micro level, what value will it add to the Macro level, and then what value will it add to the Mega level?" Without this formal link, we might have splinters of results for diverse individuals and small groups that never get synthesized or integrated to add value both within the organization and outside of it. Would you want that for your own organization? What impact would that ultimately have on the health of the organization, and each of its members? Wouldn't you want to ensure your organization is healthy so that it can continue to add value to your customers, to the community, and to you?

Be aware, most conventional organizational improvement efforts limit themselves to a Micro focus and thus endanger the entire organization if those results don't add value to the entire organization and external clients. Listing the dangers of this conventional approach is not difficult; just imagine the waste in human, capital, and physical resources, as well as the self-defeating work environment it creates.

Consequences of Macro-Only Focus

Most organizations have themselves as their primary client and beneficiary, but forget that in the long term, their customers and society have to benefit in order for the organization to continue to benefit. So suppose you focus only on a commitment to:

- deliver organizational contributions that have the quality required by your external clients (Macro/Outputs)

- deliver internal results that have the quality required by your internal partners (Micro/Products)

- have efficient internal process, programs, projects, and activities (Processes)

- ensure and deliver the quality and appropriateness of the human, capital, and physical resources required (Inputs).

While Mega results are about the measurable benefits contributed to society by your organization (for example, improved quality of life), Macro results are indicated by the measurable benefits the organization reaps from what is delivered to society (for example, profits, revenue, and market share). Keep in mind, however, that the only way to sustain organizational benefits (Macro) is by assuring societal contributions (Mega).

This Macro-level scope is wider than most organizational improvement efforts but still has some major risks. You must ask the question: *Does what the organization delivers, even if the immediate client is satisfied, add value to our shared society?* For example: How many satisfied customers (in the short run) resulted from asbestos insulation to only regret their choice a few years later? How many people were happy with fast food cooked in saturated fats, only to battle health problems later? How many people were happy with business practices in Wall Street until the stock market crash in 2008? Adding measurable value to our society is not to be assumed, it should be included in the needs assessment so sensible organizational contributions can be defined and justified.

When you examine the stated objectives of major (and your own) organizations, you will see that at best, they focus on their well-being (be the best, show a profit, highest market share, and so forth); but interestingly, these statements of purposes for organizations lack precision and rigor on how to measure their accomplishments (Kaufman, Stith, and Kaufman, 1992). That is, they are vague and provide inadequate guidance for the organization as to where it's headed and how to know when goals are reached.

These statements also lack what value the organization will add to our shared society, the assumption being that just as long as the organization is making money (or getting funded, for a public organization) it is doing well. And that limitation is the organization's Achilles' heel (Kaufman, 2010). If an organization doesn't add value to both its external clients and our shared society it will, sooner or later, falter (Davis, 2005).

Interestingly, and sadly for most organizations, the conventional wisdom is about a focus on the "bottom line" and most business cases limit themselves to the Macro/Output level

(Bernardez, 2009). That does not have to be. This point cannot be stressed enough. Making money is not a bad thing, but using it as the only and ultimate goal is not strategic. Most business-case models, unfortunately, stop at Macro. In a for-profit organization, making money is a consequence of adding value to external clients and our shared society. If the organization is driven by Mega/societal focus, it will, as a consequence, do well at the Macro/organizational level.

Results of Adding Mega/Outcomes to Focus

While most organizations ignore it, assume it, or disdain it, any organization that intends to thrive must add value to all stakeholders, including our shared society (Moore, Ellsworth, and Kaufman, 2011). A secret to organizational improvement and success is adding a focus on external clients and society to its overall purpose; adding and integrating Mega.

We all depend on other organizations and individuals to look after our survival, well-being, and quality of life. When we buy and use a car, fly in an airplane, get on a bus, eat in a restaurant, or buy groceries, we want to assume that our health and safety comes first—before their profits. When we go to a dentist, undergo surgery, or buy medicine, we want to be assured of our safety, survival, and quality of life. When we buy appliances, install new equipment, and buy electronics and cell phones, we want to be assured of our safety, survival, and quality of life when using them. Exploding airplanes, cars, and appliances are not what we or anybody else wants.

So, when we are designing and delivering anything to our external clients, should they not expect the same from us? Should not what we use, do, produce, and deliver add measurable value to them and to our shared world? Contributing measurable societal value added, as we have noted earlier, is not only practical and ethical, but also a basic requirement for strategic organizations. Not doing so is a death sentence for organizations.

Results of Adding Societal Focus

Unique to the approach in this book is including a focus on societal value added for all stakeholders. When we view our work and contributions from a *system* view, then all parts working independently and together must add value for all. By a primary (but not exclusive) focus on society—Mega—that obligation will be fulfilled.

As we will see in chapter 3, the societal level of results is defined by an *Ideal Vision*. This Ideal Vision defines the perfect future we wish to reach, and provides long-term guidance for

Figure 2.2   Alignment Between Ideal Vision, Mission, and Functions

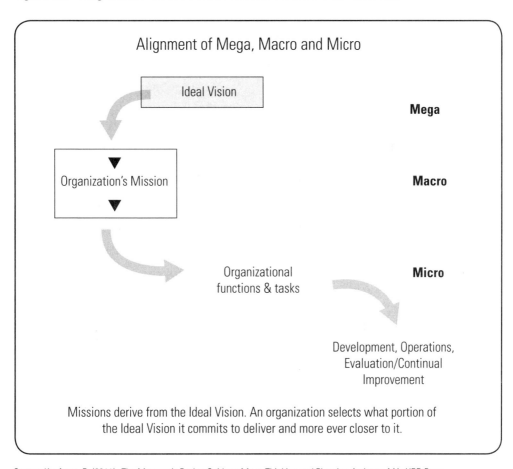

Source: Kaufman, R. (2011). *The Manager's Pocket Guide to Mega Thinking and Planning.* Amherst, MA: HRD Press.

how the organization adds value to external clients and society. Figure 2.2 illustrates the foundational role that the Ideal Vision serves in creating direction and establishing the organization's mission, functions, tasks, and means.

This societal focus—in measurable performance terms—is missing from most formulations (Moore, Ellsworth, and Kaufman, 2008, 2011; Moore, 2010). Most of those who do include a societal value added do it reactively, that is, they may identify if what they are doing happens to have a positive impact on society. That reactive mode is a good start, but not good enough; it does not purposely, efficiently, and effectively drive what the organizations uses, does, produces, and delivers inside and outside of itself. We urge that your approach to needs assessment identifies the gaps between current and desired results so that a performance bridge can and will be built to improve our shared world, and guarantee your organization's long-term survival and well-being. It is proactive and moves to improve our world using our organizations as a vehicle in a mutually beneficial way (Bernardez, 2005; 2009; Bernardez, et al., in press). If it is not adding value to our external clients and society, what do you have in mind? When making decisions, you should ask this question: *Will this add value to all internal and external stakeholders?* If not, revisit your decision criteria.

Societal Focus and Making Money Are Not at Odds

We expect everyone we deal with to put our health and safety number one on their priority list. And we should do the same for them. Think for a moment about the organizations that you do business with regularly, both in work and in life. Are you willing to allow any to put their profits or conventional objectives, above your survival, health, and well-being? Your grocery store? Your school? Your child's school? Your family physician? Your auto manufacturer?

We demand of any organization we deal with that they put us—our survival, self-sufficiency, and safety—ahead of anything on their agenda. And the same goes for your job and your organization: Others depend upon you putting them at the top of your priority list. Doing so is both practical and ethical.

If you don't add value to our shared world and our clients, you might be subtracting value. You only have to look at the wreckage of selfish organizations worldwide in the last 30 years to see that greed sooner or later catches up with them. Actually, most people are a bit surprised, at first, to find that they already contribute to Mega—and contribute much more than they initially thought.

Our success hinges on relating everything we use, do, produce, and deliver and relying on it all to add value to our shared society. If we don't, we develop only a part of something and are missing a large part of its potential contribution.

OEM and Levels of Needs Assessment

Figure 2.3 provides a conceptual view of the different levels of needs assessment. In order for you to use the right level of needs assessment for your situation, it is important to understand when to use them. Table 2.3 provides a job aid for needs assessment selection that links the various levels of needs assessments to the conditions that are associated with each of them, along with a comparison of other well-known front-end models. It also attempts to highlight their link to an analysis function that is part of a complete front-end approach.

Figure 2.3   OEM Levels of Needs Assessment

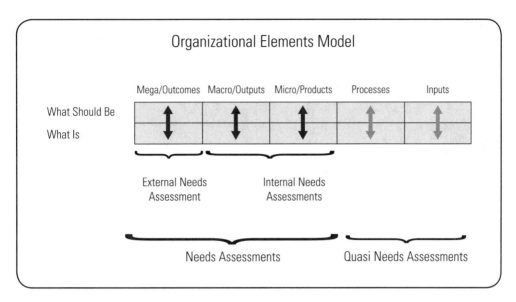

Source: Kaufman, R. (2006). *Changes, Choices, and Consequences: A Guide to Mega Thinking and Planning.* Amherst, MA: HRD Press.

Note: We will continue to use this figure of the OEM to demonstrate specific links to all levels of needs assessment and planning.

You will notice that the OEM is the only framework that has an explicit focus on external contributions to external clients and society (Mega). As you move down the OEM levels, we find that Rummler's Anatomy of Performance (AOP) is another useful framework that encompasses all the levels beneath it (Rummler, 2004). Rummler saw the organization as an adapting and processing system that must align processes, jobs, and performers to organizational objectives. The link to the external system was implicit in what he called the organizational context (for example, regulations, industry, suppliers, etc.) and ultimate value-added deliverable to external clients. However, there was no formal reference to the organization's survival and long-term success to its contributions to society. The further down the organizational levels you get, the more models we find that incorporate them as a focus in their approach. It is important to note that these are all useful models, for their intended purposes. Much of the utility of these, or any, tools depends on whether they are used for the right purpose and implemented in a thoughtful way. What we want to highlight is that you must understand the boundaries of each of the models to select the most useful for your situation.

It is also important to note that any of these models could be used in conjunction with one another or modified for the application of one comprehensive model. For example, the OEM and AOP

Table 2.3   Needs Assessment Levels and Frameworks

Level of Needs Assessment	Use It When the Organization	Relevant Needs Assessment Models	Analysis Capability

Mega	• Recognizes that what they use, do, produce, and deliver should be aligned and add value to internal and external clients, including society
	• Wants to ensure long-term survival and profitability
	• Is engaged in a strategic planning process
	• Adopts an ongoing strategic thinking culture
	• Is faced with significant change, threat, or opportunity
		• Kaufman's OEM	• Kaufman's OEM uses a series of analysis tools to further understand gaps and solution requirements.
			• See chapter 7 for a description of these analysis tools:
			  • *Cost-Consequences*
			  • *Methods-Means*
			  • *SWOT*

Macro	• Recognizes that what they use, do, produce, and deliver should be aligned and add value to internal and external clients • Assumes (rather than ensures) what it delivers to clients adds value to them • Wants to ensure profitability in the short-term • Is engaged in a tactical planning process	• Kaufman's OEM • Rummler's AOP	• Rummler's AOP depicts a comprehensive analysis process that links the organizational or business issues to critical job issues and critical process issues, including causal factors.
Micro	• Recognizes that what the organizations uses, does, and produces should be aligned and add value to internal stakeholders • Assumes (rather than ensures) that what is produced adds value to the organization and beyond • Introduces changes that will have an impact on job requirements • Is experiencing challenging symptoms related to particular jobs or performers • Is engaged in operational planning	• Kaufman's OEM • Rummler's AOP • Harless' FEA • Mager & Pipe's model	• Harless's FEA depicts a comprehensive analysis process that links human performance gaps to causal factors. • The Mager and Pipe model helps link human performance gaps to causal factors, and potential solutions.
Quasi	• Recognizes that what the organizations uses and does should be aligned • Assumes (rather than ensures) that what is used and done within the organization adds value to internal stakeholders and beyond • Is experiencing challenging symptoms related to processes or resources • Is about to implement a new process or resource • Is engaged in resource planning	• Kaufman's OEM • Rummler's AUP • Gilbert's BEM • Harless' FEA • Rossett's TNA • Mager & Pipe's model	• Gilbert's BEM is used after human performance gaps have already been identified and offers a systematic approach for analyzing causal factors contributing to those gaps, and potential solution requirements. • Rossett's TNA is primarily focused with analyzing training requirements, once training has already been identified as the required solution through a needs assessment.

Figure 2.4   Needs Assessment Selection Algorithm

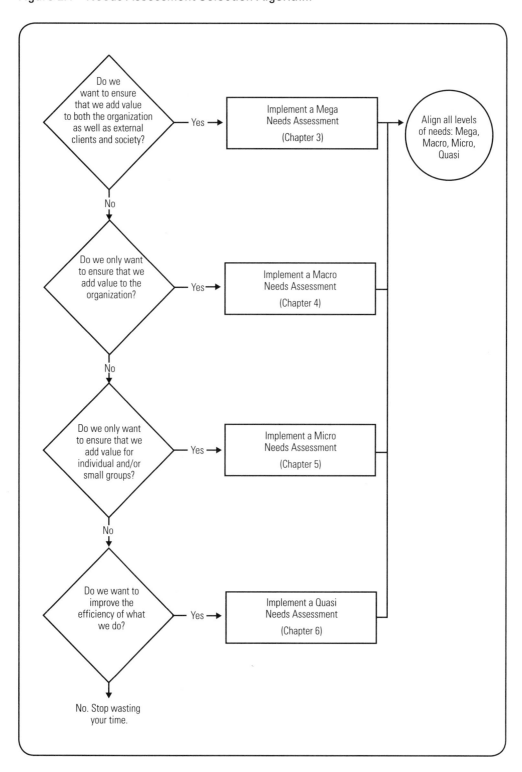

have been successfully integrated to leverage both sets of strengths, particularly the OEM's strategic societal focus, with the AOP's articulated process for linking all other organizational subsystems, such as critical business issues, critical job issues, and critical process issues.

Likewise, it is not difficult to imagine that integrating any of the needs assessment models with any specific model that more heavily focuses on analysis would offer a powerful tool for assessing and analysis performance gaps.

Figure 2.4 (on the previous page) provides an algorithm to help you select the appropriate level of needs assessment, directing your attention to the respective chapter of this book.

Each of the Organizational Elements are equally important and must be linked and aligned. While most planning and needs assessment approaches focus on one or two—but omit Mega—all must be formally, rigorously, and measurably considered. Organizational success depends on adding measurable value both within and outside of the organization and this must be done by all who commit to success.

Chapter Summary

In this chapter, you learned about the OEM, and its role as a framework for conducting needs assessments that systemically link all organizational levels, as well as aligning internal and external results and consequences. We also discussed the importance of starting with societal value added as the anchor for conducting needs assessments, and the potential risks of assuming external value added.

Chapter 3
Performing a Mega-Level Needs Assessment

What's in This Chapter?

- Why you should include societal value added in needs assessment and planning

- How to conduct an "organizational front-end aligned" Mega-level needs assessment

- Determining your vision and mission by identifying an Ideal Vision and related Vital Signs

- Prioritizing needs—gaps in results—and costs

Why do some organizations get into trouble? One basic reason they fail, along with professionals' attempts at performance improvement, is the failure to link everything to useful external results and impacts. In automotive terms, what is suggested here is more like front-end alignment than front-end analysis. As one of the fathers of measurable objectives once noted, "If you don't know where you are headed, you might end up someplace else" (Mager, 1997).

Mega-level needs assessment provides the essential "front-end alignment" that ensures that everything an organization and performance improvement professionals do is linked—from resources to activities to products to delivery to external impact: linking Inputs, Processes, Products, Outputs, and Outcomes.

Let's see what is really involved in doing a needs assessment at the Mega level, which identifies and justifies what value should be added to our organization as well as to our shared world. Central to a Mega-level needs assessment is the Organizational Elements Model, Figure 3.1. The case study scenario that follows the model illustration demonstrates this concept.

Figure 3.1   Organizational Elements Model

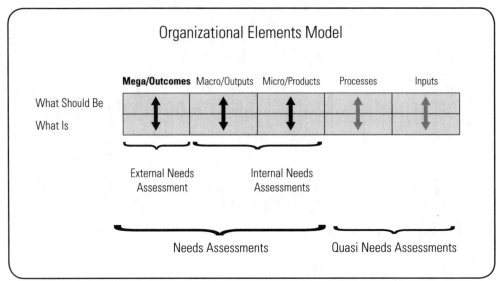

Source: Kaufman, R., 2006.

Case Study Scenario

The Bewell Insurance Company (BIC) employs approximately 5,000 employees. The health-care provider has a reputation for being a leader in the marketplace because of its customer focus, but also having higher rates than competitors. In addition, the healthcare industry is about to experience a radical change for group customers, individual members, and em-ployees because of a National Health Reform. Soon, all individuals will be mandated to have health insurance, either through their employer or by using the newly formed Health-care Exchange. The healthcare industry will have more of a retail focus. As a result, it is imperative that BIC acts strategically to not only grow business and maintain the existing business, but also maintain its reputation as a healthcare provider that puts the health and well-being of its subscribers first and demonstrates superior health results.

BIC's vice president has just contacted you to assist in identifying strategies for capitalizing on relevant new legislation and ensuring that BIC's current and future customers continue to be satisfied with products and services that meet their health and quality of life needs.

How do you proceed?

Why Conduct a Mega-Level Assessment

A Mega-level needs assessment is a process for identifying and resolving gaps between the desired and actual accomplishments and contributions of an organization, as measured by the usefulness and value of those accomplishments to the organization's external clients and our shared society. Relevant accomplishments at this level, for any type of organization, may relate to economic and personal security, public health, safety, environmental impact, quality of life, and survival.

Societal value added—measurable value added—is required for success. Unique to the approach in this book is the focus on societal value added for all stakeholders. When we view our work and contributions through a *system view*, then all parts of the organization are working independently and together to achieve a common purpose—they must add value for all. By a primary (but not exclusive) focus on society—Mega—that obligation will be fulfilled. Doing so is both practical and ethical (Moore, 2010). As we explained in chapter 2, this societal focus is missing from most formulations, which is why we urge that your approach identifies the gaps between current and desired results. This proactive approach works to the benefit of all.

A systemic needs assessment is then ideally conducted at each level, in sequence, from Mega to Macro to Micro, as shown in Figure 3.2.

The five levels of organizational elements—Mega, Macro, Micro, Processes, and Inputs—must be defined with rigor and precision, and they must also relate one to the others so whatever you use, do, produce, and deliver will add value to your external clients and society. This primary (but not exclusive) attention to Mega—societal value added—is vital, measurable, and missing from most other approaches to needs assessment and planning. The Ideal Vision, described later in this chapter, provides the variables that compose Mega, and those variables should be included in any needs assessment.

When to Use Mega-Level Assessment

While the Mega level is always relevant and should be the basis for all organizational improvement efforts, a Mega-level needs assessment is particularly appropriate when the organization finds itself in any of the following scenarios:

- recognizes that what they use, do, produce, and deliver should be aligned and add measurable value to internal and external clients, including society

Figure 3.2   Link Between Mega, Macro, and Micro Needs Assessments

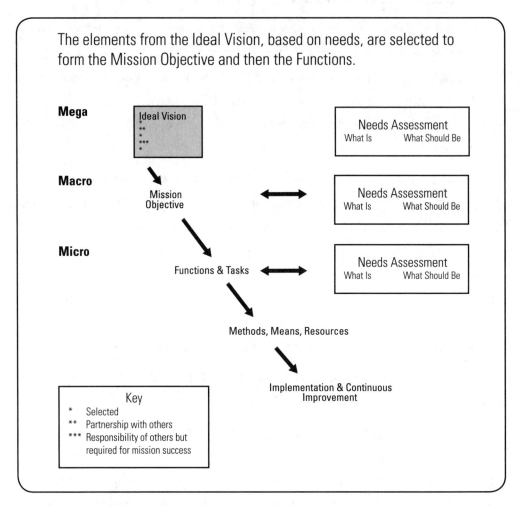

Source: Based on Kaufman, R., 2000, 2006, and 2011.

- has a primary focus on creating the world we want for future generations

- wants to ensure long-term survival and profitability or funding

- is engaged in a strategic planning process

- adopts an ongoing strategic thinking culture

- is faced with significant change, threat, or opportunity.

For example, in the BIC scenario, the organization is facing a significant change with the new legislature, which essentially changes the marketplace for healthcare providers. This change is significant enough to warrant a careful look at the organization's vision, strategic direction, and relevant gaps between where they are and where they want to go.

Process for Conducting

The scope of a needs assessment at this level requires a focus on identifying gaps in terms of the contribution to the survival, self-sufficiency, and quality of life of the organization's external clients and society. Figure 3.3 provides an overview of the process for conducting a Mega-level needs assessment. You will recognize that it follows the same general steps as those presented in chapter 2, with Mega-level contextualization.

Figure 3.3   Mega-Level Needs Assessment Process

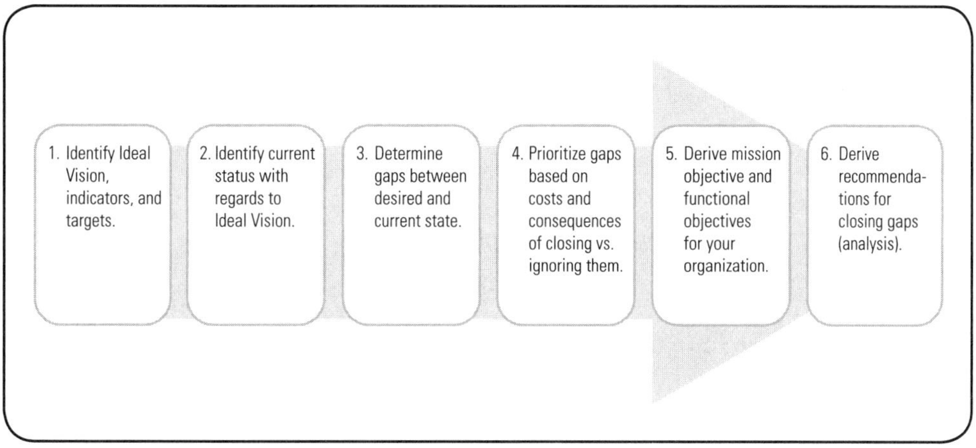

Step 1—Identify Ideal Vision and Associated Indicators (or Vital Signs and Targets)

A vision states the kind of world we want to create together, for future generations using organizations and individuals as the vehicle.

Mega is defined by an *Ideal Vision*. An Ideal Vision is ideal; it defines where we should be headed even though we might not get there tomorrow, next month, next year, or in the next decade. It is a worthy destination to set for any conscientious and truly strategic organization.

> **The Ideal Vision:** *There will be no losses of life, elimination, or reduction of levels of well-being, survival, self-sufficiency, or quality of life from any source.*

While not every organization will be responsible, either alone or with others, for all of the Ideal Vision, each organization identifies which variables it commits to deliver and move ever-closer toward through its product or service. The vision does not imply that an organization change its line of work (unless of course it truly doesn't add value to its clients and society); rather, it implies the direction an organization should strive for through its products or service if it is to be truly valued by its clients and society.

A product or service that that is worthwhile should not only add financial value to the organization, but should also add value to the survival and quality of life of its internal and external clients. What else would make your customers loyal to your organization? Would you continue to buy cars from an automotive company that sold vehicles that were defective and dangerous? Would you continue to eat at a restaurant where you got food poisoning? Would you continue to bank at a financial institution that adds hidden fees, and engages in discriminatory lending practices based on gender, age, race, or other irrelevant variables?

Everything we use, do, produce, and deliver must add value at the societal level (a "system approach").

Organizational Vital Signs

In much the same way as our physicians check our blood pressure, weight, and blood chemistry to determine our overall health and what we might do to improve it, the elements in the Ideal Vision may be used to check the health of one's organization. Ideal Vision indicators—*Vital Signs*—of success are broken down into two levels.

First level—basic survival for all people:

- Zero pollution—there is no permanent destruction of our environment.

- No deaths or permanent disabilities result from what is delivered.

- No starvation and/or malnutrition resulting in death or incapacity.

- No partner or spouse abuse resulting in death or incapacitating physical or psychological damage.

- No disease or disabilities resulting in death or incapacity.

- No substance abuse resulting in death or incapacity.

- No murder, rape, crimes of violence, robbery, fraud, or destruction of property.

- No war, riot, or terrorism, or civil unrest resulting in death or incapacity of individuals or groups.

- No accidents resulting in death or incapacity.

- Citizens achieve and maintain a positive qualify of life.

Second level—organizational survival that will result from meeting level one Vital Signs (Ideal Outcomes):

- There is continued funding or profits based on measurable and demonstrated positive return on investment.

- No successful lawsuits sustained against the organization for defective or inappropriate products or services.

- Programs, projects, activities, and operations meet all performance objectives while not violating first-tier requirements.

These are indeed ideal. We might not deliver them all now or even soon, but this list provides a common guiding star for our strategic planning and ethical compass toward which we may continually move. The Vital Signs are best taken together rather than in a splintered way so that the relationships can be made clear.

This is not the conventional wisdom. The old paradigm was "the business of business is business" and "what's good for our company is good for the world." Or "the bottom line is our most important concern" and "we look after the business, and the government looks after the people." This is self-absorbed, and totally out of touch with reality. We only have to look at the wreckage of organizations (big ones) that have failed by following the conventional models or approaches: Lehman Brothers, Washington Mutual, WorldCom, General Motors, CIT, Enron, Conseco, Chrysler, Pacific Gas and Electric, Financial Corporation of America, UAL-United Air Lines, Delta Air Lines, Tribune Company, Swiss Air, Woolworths, and more, possibly including entire cities, counties, and countries that face default.

Each failing organization neglected to put the survival and self-sufficiency of their clients and our shared society at the center of its planning and needs assessment. They followed incomplete models and "false prophets."

You can and should do better. Your career and your organization's survival depend on it, just as you depend on this from all organizations and people with which you deal. This has become so important that more and more major organizations are moving toward Mega.

It is vital to our success that we look beyond the conventional boundaries of planning and doing, look beyond "the usual business case" or "the quarterly profits"—beyond any one organization, division, department, or group. Our success hinges on our relating everything we use, do, produce, and deliver on adding value to our shared society—our world, our universe. If we don't, we develop only a part of the whole and not the entire whole.

When making decisions, ask, "Will this add value to all internal and external stakeholders?" If not, revisit your decision criteria. Remember, all organizations share the Ideal Vision and the Vital Signs. A responsive organization will select, on the basis of the results of a needs assessment, what Vital Signs they commit to address and move ever closer to meeting.

The chapter 11 Tool Kit provides exercises to use to clarify and come to agreement on the Ideal Vision and Vital Signs and their role in needs assessment and planning.

Vision and Mission Options—All Related to Mega

We recommend that the mission of any organization is based on the Vital Signs indicators chosen (based on needs and priorities). The other option is to first derive an "organizational vision" that is also based on the selected Vital Signs.

What if an organization wants to derive its own vision? It is conventional in much of the literature that each organization should have its own vision and mission. We urge that for simplicity's sake that all organizations strive toward the one Ideal Vision presented earlier in this chapter, and its associated Vital Signs as a common guiding star. Some planners are more comfortable with creating their own vision that is more of a targeted version of the Ideal Vision. If this is the case, then the "organizational vision" should be based on results at the Mega level, and should best target those Vital Signs that the organization has selected as relevant to them. Regardless of choosing the ideal vision or tailoring one's own organizational vision, ensure that each links to societal needs and requirements.

Creating Your Organization's Vision

You may recall from previous chapters that stakeholders are an integral part of a needs assessment process; they must feel that they are active stakeholders, as they should be. To create the organization's vision you must have their participation, inputs, and buy-in. The Mega rationale previously provided in this book will be useful to that end.

For example, to determine the vision for the Bewell Insurance Company (BIC) (refer to the scenario at the beginning of this chapter), coordinate a meeting (or perhaps multiple meetings) with a representative group of stakeholders who are affected by BIC's accomplishments and how it operates, such as:

- top executive team and key board members

- representative group of current clients

- representative group of the community

- representative group of strategic partners, including representative employees.

These individuals will become the needs assessment and planning team. Their first task will be to essentially define the organization's mission. In other words, they will establish What Should Be.

The mission will be determined through facilitated discussions until a consensus is reached about what elements and Vital Signs from the Ideal Vision truly represent the added-value future toward which the organization wants to contribute. It will provide a measurable statement of where the organization is headed, how it will know what progress it is making, and what to change and what to revise as they move from What Is to What Should Be.

Back to our example, for BIC, the relevant primary elements might be:

- *Disease:* As a healthcare provider, they have direct influence on disease treatment and avoidance. They provide not only medical treatment for disease, but have the ability to influence behavior through information and services related to healthy living.

- *Substance abuse:* As other diseases, BIC cannot only provide products that support proper treatment of substance abuse, but can also provide information and services that help identify early warning signs and prevent substance abuse (for example, its Parent and Adolescent Drug Prevention Program).

- *Physical abuse:* Under the new legislation, screening for domestic abuse for women will be made available free of charge.

- *Accidents:* Here as well, BIC provides preventive informational programs for customers. Also, it has direct influence on avoiding unnecessary accidents for BIC employees in their own workplace.

- *Because of what BIC uses, does, produces, and delivers there will be no successful lawsuits stemming from what the organization provides.* This is an indicator of organizational health and sustainability.

- *Discrimination based on irrelevant factors:* BIC enforces policies that ensure that health plan coverage rules are equitably enforced across gender, age, race, ethnicity, and other irrelevant factors. Likewise, it can do so in its hiring practices.

Specific indicators for each of these ideal vision elements, and their ideal targets might look like those shown in Table 3.1.

Table 3.1   Sample Indicators for BIC Scenario

Ideal Vision Element	Indicators (and Ideal Targets)
Disease	• No customers are diagnosed with avoidable crippling diseases.
Substance abuse	• No customers abuse substances.
Physical abuse	• No customers are physically abused.
Accidents	• No employees are injured due to avoidable accidents in the workplace.
Successful lawsuits	• There are no adverse legal judgments.
Discrimination based on irrelevant factors	• There are no complaints of discrimination.

The organizational vision for BIC might read something like this:

BIC will create a future where no customers are diagnosed with avoidable crippling diseases, including substance abuse, and are not discriminated against on the basis of irrelevant variables. Its employees will enjoy a good quality of life through fair compensation and a healthy and safe work environment.

Because they all point in the same direction, Ideal Visions tend to have similar characteristics across organizations, and consistently include the types of indicators you saw in the Ideal Vision and the Vital Signs described above (Figure 3.1). Table 3.2 provides examples from different sectors.

Vital Signs

Notice each organizational mission listed above is focused on Mega elements found in the Ideal Vision and Vital Signs. Examples include graduate self-sufficiency, error-free life-saving treatments, and unbiased access to financial and local development opportunities for all. There is no emphasis on "how" the visions will be achieved. Where references are made to core elements of an organization (such as "life-saving innovations"), a qualifier that relates it back to a Mega result can also be found. While all of the focus should be placed on results, it is important to note that the needs assessment partners must feel ownership over their vision. Sometimes, this means being able to recognize key attributes of their organizational identity in that vision. What is critical is that when it comes to establishing measurable indicators of the Ideal Vision, that they are valid indicators of Mega results.

Table 3.2   Examples of Organizational Missions Based on the Ideal Vision

Institution	Mission
Financial	Ensure the continued success of our organization while measurably improving the quality of life of the community by providing customers with unbiased access to accurate, responsive, and responsible financial solutions, without regard to irrelevant variables such as race, color, religion, ethnic background, gender, and sexual orientation.
Medical	We will be the most innovative and dependable healthcare system in the country through our primary concern for the health and well-being of our patients, record of error-free treatment, and life-saving innovations within the financial resources of our patients.
Educational	We will prepare students to become self-sufficient and self-reliant contributing members of society.
Non-Governmental Organization (NGO)	Assure the attainment of local development that benefits all citizens, ensuring fair participation across genders, generations, and ethnic groups.

As you can see, the Ideal Vision is quite relevant and a practical basis for any organizational mission that is truly strategic; it will ensure the organization's long-term survival based on adding value to its external customers and society.

Here is an overview of how to create a vision for your organization:

- Form a needs assessment partnership that includes top executives and decision makers, clients, strategic business partners, community partners.

- Coordinate a retreat-type working meeting with needs assessment partners, in an interruption-free environment.

- Facilitate a participatory discussion that helps the partners define their vision in measurable results terms, rechanneling discussions of "means" for another time (including methods-means analysis, to be discussed in chapter 7). Get agreement on what parts of the Ideal Vision and Vital Signs they and the organization commit to deliver. This agreement should be based on needs assessment data for each of the Vital Signs.

- Define measurable indicators and ideal targets for the organization mission results.

Step 2—Identify Current Status as Related to Ideal Vision

The essence of this process is collecting data on the same variables that were selected as essential to the organization's vision, based on the Ideal Vision and Vital Signs.

It is not unusual for some of that data to not currently exist, or not yet be feasible to collect. In these cases, it is possible that the specific indicator can be further subdivided into other relevant metrics that measure different dimensions of that indicator. In some cases, those metrics will be picked because they are relevant and the organization already collects that data, or because they can be found in some public or private domain.

For example, two of the variables that BIC selected as relevant to their vision were disease and drug abuse. See Table 3.3 for how these might be further subdivided.

While in the previous step, the partners set ideal targets for those indicators, here, the partners (or a technical subgroup) will lead the data collection effort to determine the current status of those indicators. In other words, establish the What Is. Because the data is not likely to be readily available, this step is not likely to be completed during the retreat used to identify the Ideal Vision.

Table 3.3   Breakdown of Mega-Level Indicators for BIC

Ideal Vision Vital Signs Element	Indicators (and Ideal Targets)	Subdivided Into
• Disease	• No customers are diagnosed with avoidable crippling diseases.	• Number of female customers of target age who are screened regularly for breast cancer • Number of male customers of target age who are regularly screened for prostate cancer • Number of customers who are subscribed to our nutrition and exercise program who are morbidly obese
• Drug Abuse	• No customers abuse substances.	• Number of professionally treated customers that are reportedly drug-free after three years.
• Physical abuse	• No customers are physically abused.	• Number of women who are screened for physical abuse • Number of women who are reportedly out of physically abusive conditions beyond a two-year period

Determining Current Status

The data you collect must be directly related to the indicators you identified for measuring the Ideal Vision. The data can be:

- *Hard:* Independently verifiable facts and figures; examples include profit over time, diagnosed diseases, or lawsuits.

- *Soft:* Personal perceptions of individuals; for example, perceived needs, opinions, beliefs, or values.

The Internet and advances in technologies allow us to link to reports, documents, data-bases, experts, and other sources not previously possible. For example, social indicators such as those related to quality of life (average income levels, divorce rates, crime levels, and the like) can often be found in Chambers of Commerce archives, census reports, police records, and community quality of life reports, many of which are available electronically. Others, such as those related to the environment (pollution, corporate toxic waste, to name a couple), could be obtained from the Environmental Protection Agency (EPA), as well as from studies published in scientific journals. A number of other government agencies and research institutions, nationally and internationally, also publish a series of official studies and reports that could prove to be valuable sources of data.

In many cases, you can find the data that you are looking for within the organization itself. Existing records about past and current performance may already be available, but collected by different parties in your organization and for different reasons. Be sure to thoroughly search for these potential sources, as it could save valuable time, money, and other resources. If data do not exist, note that and realize that future work should collect it.

Then, use the appropriate data collection tools considering the type of data you are seeking, and the source of that data. For example, if you are looking for individuals' anonymous self-reports of drug abuse, then an anonymous online questionnaire might be appropriate. If, however, you are looking for formal reports of discrimination, doing an extant data review of existing documentation of discrimination complaints would be more appropriate.

There are plenty of useful data collection books and other resources, so data collection details will not be covered here; however, we do provide an overview of methodological consid-erations in chapter 8. Additionally, Guerra-López (2007, 2008) provides concrete information on data collection and analysis methodology. The product of the data collection effort for the BIC might look something like what is illustrated in Table 3.4.

Step 3—Determine Gap Between Desired and Current State

This step in essence clarifies the difference between What Should Be and What Is with regard to the Ideal Vision. Take a look at Table 3.5 for an example of these gaps, based on the BIC scenario.

We want to clarify the total gaps between ideal and real. This is important because we do not want establish fictitious targets that are not based on reality—that is like building a tall and heavy structure over quicksand. All planning, design, and development must be based on solid ground if it is going to be useful.

Table 3.4   Current Status as Compared to the Ideal Vision and Vital Signs

BIC Vital Signs: What Should Be	Current Status Signs: What Is
• No customers are diagnosed with avoidable crippling diseases.	• 87% of our female customers of target age are screened regularly for breast cancer. • 79% of our male customers of target age are regularly screened for prostate cancer. • Of those customers who take advantage of our nutrition and exercise program, 32% report they are clinically obese.
• No customers abuse substances.	• Of those receiving treatment, 72% are reportedly drug-free after three years.
• No customers are physically abused.	• 80% of women registering for physical abuse screening actually get screened. • 68% of women are reportedly out of physically abusive conditions beyond a two-year period.
• No employees are victims of unavoidable accidents in the workplace.	• Four employees suffered injuries due to avoidable accidents on the job last year.
• There are no complaints of discrimination.	• Two lawsuits were filed by customers for discrimination in the last three years.

This does not mean that your organization is committing to reaching 100 percent of anything at the end of this month, quarter, year, or even next year. We are primarily using this as a basis for clarifying reality to all needs assessment and planning partners and strategically addressing these gaps over time. Typical strategic planning—real strategic planning—has a horizon of at least 10 years. Even then, success is not necessarily determined by a yes or no answer to closing gaps, rather, by successive approximations toward that desired destination. Later in this chapter we will discuss the process for establishing the mission objective and subsequent functional aims based on this realistic, and sometimes difficult, view of real gaps.

Finally, another benefit of clarifying the gaps this way is that when the mission objective is communicated to the rest of the organization and the world, closing these gaps will not seem out of reach. In other words, to an organizational member responsible for preventing injuries in the BIC workplace, a reduction of four seems like a more feasible accomplishment than reaching an absolute "zero" point. Psychologically, this will be challenging enough to keep them moving forward, but not so unreachable that it renders them immobile with skepticism.

Table 3.5   BIC Mega-Level Gaps

BIC Vital Signs: What Should Be	Current Status: What Is	Gap
• No customers are diagnosed with avoidable crippling diseases.	• 87% of our female customers of target age are screened regularly for breast cancer. • 79% of our male customers of target age are regularly screened for prostate cancer. • Of those customers who take advantage of our nutrition and exercise program, 32% report they are clinically obese.	• 13% (based on wanting 100% of them to be screened regularly, and increase chances of early detection and treatment) • 21% (based on an ideal target of 100% of customers getting regularly screened) • 32% (based on an ideal target of no customers being morbidly obese; obesity leads to many otherwise avoidable diseases.)
• No customers abuse substances	• Of those receiving treatment, 72% are reportedly drug-free after three years.	• 28% (based on an ideal target of 100% successfully in recovery from drug abuse)
• No customers are physically abused.	• 80% of women registering for physical abuse screening actually get screened. • 68% of women are reportedly out of physically abusive conditions beyond a two-year period.	• 20% (based on an ideal target of 100% for screening follow-through) • 32% (based on an ideal target of 100% for permanent abuse recovery)
• No employees are victims of unavoidable accidents in the workplace.	• Four employees suffered injuries due to avoidable accidents on the job last year.	• Four injuries (based on an ideal target of no avoidable accidents in the BIC workplace)
• There are no complaints of discrimination.	• Two lawsuits filed by customers for discrimination in the last three years.	• Two lawsuits (based on an ideal target of no lawsuits for discrimination)

Step 4— Prioritize Gaps Based on Cost and Consequences of Closing Gaps vs. Ignoring Them

Not all gaps are of the same importance or urgency. Those considered most important, and in some cases, most urgent, should be addressed first. The planning partners will have to make decisions about which to address first. Needs assessors can support those decisions by clarifying the relative importance of those gaps in a facilitated discussion with planning partners based on a series of criteria, including:

- *Magnitude:* Some gaps will be larger than others and could be perceived to be of high priority. Of course, this doesn't mean that the largest gaps are by default more critical than others.

- *Costs and consequences:* The costs (financial and nonfinancial) of one gap might be greater than for others, even its magnitude isn't as big as others. In our BIC example, we have a gap of "four accidents in the workplace," and while the magnitude or size of this gap is not as large as the 28 percent gap in customers who successfully recover from drug abuse, it does not make it any less important. In both cases, people's lives are at stake. So both bring a great human cost and consequence.

- *Organizational resources and capital (financial and nonfinancial):* While we would not recommend that these criteria take precedence of costs, consequences, and magnitude, the realities in which the organizational partners live with force us to consider these elements, including political will. At the very least, the prioritization discussion should include some reference to this as a matter of context or climate.

Be open to other criteria that the needs assessment and planning partners may consider important. Our experience tells us that most useful criteria will fall under "costs and conse-quences." However, being receptive to needs assessment and planning partners' ideas is impor-tant for buy-in and continued active participation.

Priority Categories

Some general categories of priority order could include:

- **High priority:** Carries large costs and consequences associated with ignoring the need at this point in time.

- **Moderate priority:** Carries some costs and consequences associated with ignoring the need at this point in time.

- **Low priority:** Carries minimal costs and consequences associated with ignoring the need at this or at a later time.

The end result of a prioritization session for BIC might look something like Table 3.6. While the BIC needs assessment and planning partners considered all of these important, the discussion led them to believe that the health-related issues were most critical and central to their "reason for being" as a healthcare provider. They then agreed to address these gaps as an integral part of their strategy and tactics.

Addressing these gaps as a central part of organizational strategy is different from having a corporate social responsibility initiative that consists of side charitable programs. While these charitable programs have the potential to offer much wanted help to those who are unfortunate or unlucky, they are not necessarily integrated into the strategic direction and mission of the organization, and thus may not affect how it does business for the improvement of its customers and society.

For example, a tobacco company that has a charitable food program that feeds the hungry on the weekends as part of a corporate social responsibility initiative can continue to produce tobacco that contributes to the death of millions of people and still not be responsive to Mega. If, however, the company integrated the health and well-being of its customers as a core element of their strategy, this would imply changes to their products and processes. The company's research and development team might be charged with coming up with a tobacco-based product that had zero negative impact on the health and well-being of consumers.

Table 3.6   Gaps and Their Levels of Priority

Gap	Priority Level
• 13% (based on wanting 100% of them to be screened regularly, and increase chances of early detection and treatment)	• High
• 21% (based on an ideal target of 100% of customers getting regularly screened)	• High
• 32% (based on an ideal target of no customers being morbidly obese; obesity leads to many otherwise avoidable diseases.)	• High
• 28% (based on an ideal target of 100% successfully in recovery from drug abuse)	• High
• 20% (based on an ideal target of 100% for screening follow-through)	• High
• 32% (based on an ideal target of 100% for permanent abuse recovery)	• High
• Four injuries (based on an ideal target of no avoidable accidents in the BIC workplace)	• High
• Two lawsuits (based on an ideal target of no lawsuits for discrimination)	• Moderate

Step 5—Derive Mission Objective and Function Objectives

While the Ideal Vision and Vital Signs describe the ideal future, the mission objective describes a tangible, responsive, and feasible aspect of it. A mission objective specifies an achievable target accomplishment within a specific time period that will meet the identified needs. Your mission objective is based on the Ideal Vision and Vital Signs; however, it has specific measurable criteria that your organization can accomplish within your target deadline and commit to move closer toward in the future. This is usually where much conventional strategic planning starts, with some important differences: 1) there are no specific and measurable accomplishments targeted; and 2) if there are, they are not usually grounded on a Mega-level needs assessment.

Again, in collaboration with your partners, you should facilitate a meeting where they will decide how close to the Ideal Vision and Vital Signs needs the organization will come in the future, perhaps starting with a 10-year horizon, then a five-year target, then a three-year, and then next year. (Interestingly, General Motors research noted that they have a 40-year planning horizon.)

To clarify, having a 10-year horizon as an anchor for a mission objective does not imply that this objective could not become obsolete before that 10-year mark. Its purpose is to provide a

By the end of fiscal year 2023, the Bewell Insurance Company will remain as leaders in the industry by demonstrating perfect customer health records. To accomplish our mission, we will reduce the incidence of avoidable diseases through at least a 13 percent increase in early cancer detection though early screening compliance among women of target age, and at least 21 percent among men of target age. This decrease will continue until 100 percent is reached. We will also reduce heart and other obesity-related disease by a reduction of at least 32 percent in the number of customers who are morbidly obese. We will also deliver a reduction in drug abuse by increasing the number of successfully treated clients by at least 28 percent. BIC also commits to an increase of at least 20 percent in physical abuse screening for women, as well as an increase of at least 32 percent for successful recovery from physically abusive conditions. We will reduce the number of injuries suffered on the job by at least four per year until zero is reached. We will accomplish this in part by ensuring a safe work environment for our employees that will be evidenced by zero injuries in the workplace. We will consistently reduce adjudicated incidents of discrimination until the number reaches zero and remains at zero.

strategic anchor for more mid- and short-term objectives that are directed toward and linked to a long-term strategic aim. As we will see in chapter 8, needs should be tracked on an ongoing basis quite feasibly with the aid of automated performance dashboards. As you see the trends from year to year, it is quite possible that the gaps will be closed sooner than expected, or perhaps emerging needs or external circumstances will require a change in organizational direction. See the sidebar (above) to review the BIC planning partners' mission objective with a 10-year horizon.

If this is a 10-year based mission, Figure 3.4 represents what the intervals might be for the preceding years.

Definition of Function Objectives

Function objectives are elements of your mission objective that you can accomplish as the focus of your organization's business plan. They are at the Macro and Micro level and when added up and accomplished, result in the attainment of the mission objective.

Figure 3.4   One-Year Intervals of Achievement Based on 10-Year Horizon

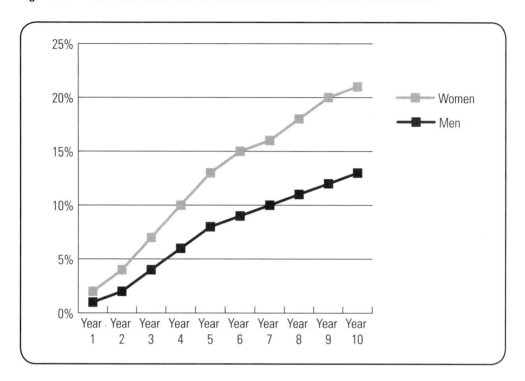

Function objectives help us break down the mission objective into more focused pieces that will become the realm of various departments, groups, and individuals of the organization. In this sense, they will help establish results-oriented realms of responsibility and accountability that are directly linked to the organization's vision and mission. They also become the basis for tactical, operational, action, and resource planning. For example, some building-block objectives for the BIC might target the following intentions:

Macro level:

- Increase market share.
- Increase profitability.
- Increase customer satisfaction.
- Increase revenue.
- Increase customer retention.
- Increase new customer acquisition.

Micro level:

- All sales and service representatives will accomplish absolute customer satisfaction.

- All sales and service representatives will demonstrate competence in handling customer changes to their coverage related to the new legislation.

- All sales and service representatives track regular cancer screening compliance for customers of target age during service calls and provide accurate information about coverage and BIC-sponsored early screening events and information.

The measurable target is not included here, because as we mentioned earlier, setting useful targets depends on the gap between ideal and current targets. That gap becomes the actual target we shoot for in the types of objectives listed above, following a similar process we used to create the mission objective.

Step 6—Derive Recommendations for Closing Gaps Based on Analysis

Useful recommendations are a byproduct of conducting a thorough, yet practical, set of analyses that include:

- *Causal analysis:* An analysis that looks at the root causes of the gaps identified during the needs assessment. These causes will provide the basic foundation for identifying solution criteria. In order for a solution to be considered, it should meet the basic solution criteria.

- *Methods-means analysis:* An analysis that provides a comparison and contrast among the various solutions under consideration, based on the criteria they meet, along with additional pros and cons for each of those solutions.

- *Cost-consequences analysis:* An analysis that looks at the costs and consequences of a given decision. The decision could be whether or not to close a gap, or whether to select one solution alternative or another. All decisions and actions (and lack thereof) come with a set of costs and consequences.

- *SWOT analysis:* An analysis of an organization's strengths, weaknesses, opportunities, and threats, with regard to a specific set of objectives. It is important to note that an organization's SWOT analysis is most useful when focused on a specific set of objectives, rather than an approach that is more general, as the SWOTs might be different for two different sets of objectives, even within one organization.

Chapter 7 provides a detailed description of each of these analyses and how to use them to make effective recommendations.

Challenges of Conducting a Mega-Level Needs Assessment

While the benefits of conducting a Mega-level needs assessment have been discussed throughout this and previous chapters, it is also important to consider some major challenges.

One of the challenges that will have to be overcome is conventional wisdom and current practice. Conventional wisdom would have us do business as usual, which at best focuses on Macro-level results such as profitability, and at worst focuses on resources and processes. To be profitable on an ongoing basis, needs assessment and planning partners must understand that sustained profitability is directly related to the value added to customers and society. Help them see this link and provide relevant examples that will help serve as evidence.

Another challenge is getting buy-in from all relevant stakeholders. While Mega will seem obvious and pragmatic to some, it will seem too far removed from the "everyday stressors" to others. Again, this is a matter of helping everyone see the relevance of Mega. Each stakeholder group has its own set of priorities and it is important that you effectively link those priorities to a Mega-level needs assessment. And perhaps through the discussion, you can also point out some additional benefits that were not previously considered.

Finally, follow-through is important. It does little good to go through the challenges of conducting a Mega-level needs assessment if the recommendations are never implemented and no real organizational change occurs. High-performing and long-standing organizations are not at the top because they are lucky, they stay at the top because they have the foresight and discipline to do all the things that they should do in order to stay there; they maintain their focus on adding value to their customers and society. Change can be difficult, but it is inevitable. We can either be the victims of it, or the creators.

Conducting a useful needs assessment depends upon the precision and rigor of what you do and how you do it. Everything that is used, done, produced, and delivered must be linked and aligned to Mega. To guide this, use the Organizational Elements Model and apply the Vital Signs for the criteria for identifying, justifying, and selecting needs—gaps in results—to be addressed.

Chapter Summary

In this chapter we discussed the importance of including societal value added in needs assessment and planning. We then presented the process for a Mega-level needs assessment and discussed each step in detail, including how to define visions and missions based on prioritized gaps.

Chapter 4
Performing a Macro-Level Needs Assessment

What's in This Chapter?

- A holistic approach to Macro-level needs assessment

- Why and when Macro-level needs assessment should be conducted

- A step-by-step guide to conducting a Macro-level needs assessment

- Updating objectives using data from the Macro-level needs assessment

- Dealing with implementation challenges

- Reinforces that starting at the Macro-level assumes that objectives link to Mega results and consequences

- In hypothetical example, walks through the steps and decisions for conduction

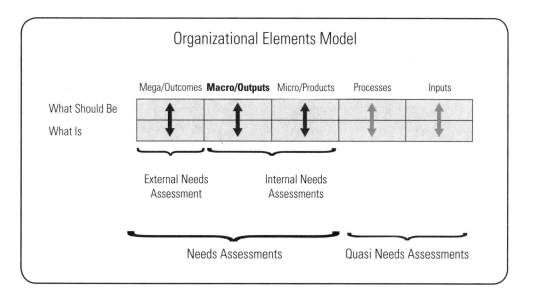

As you recall from chapter 3, Bewell Insurance Company (BIC) is facing an important change with new legislation that mandates health insurance for all United States citizens. This will have an impact at all levels of the organization; in particular, the chief operating officer's concern is to figure out how to maintain BIC's leadership in the industry, especially in terms of profitability.

Why Conduct a Macro-Level Assessment

A Macro-level needs assessment is a process for identifying and resolving gaps between the desired and actual accomplishments of an organization, as measured by organizational outputs, regardless of the value those outputs provide to external clients and society. Relevant accomplishments at this level for a company may relate to market share, revenue, sales, profits, and customer satisfaction. For a healthcare system, you might also add patient discharge. For an educational organization, it might include graduation rates, performance on national and state standardized tests, enrollment rates, retention rates, and perhaps secured funding, if it is tied to performance.

Recall that while Mega results are about the measurable benefits contributed to society by your organization (for example, improved quality of life, or longer productive life), Macro results are indicated by the measurable benefits the organization reaps from society, (for example, profits, revenue, market share). Again, the only way to sustain organizational benefits (Macro) is by assuring societal contributions (Mega).

A Macro-level needs assessment is helpful in ensuring that organizational efforts are linked to organizational and societal needs. While not a truly strategic approach (actually a tactical approach), it has the potential to improve the effectiveness and efficiency of the organization by aligning Products, Processes, and Inputs to organizational Outputs. Strategic effectiveness can only be influenced if a Mega-level needs assessment is conducted prior to the Macro-level needs assessment.

When to Use a Macro-Level Assessment

Like Mega, the Macro level is always relevant and should be considered for all organizational improvement efforts, a Macro-level needs assessment is particularly appropriate when the organization faces any of the following scenarios:

- recognizes that what they use, do, produce, and deliver should be aligned and add value to internal and external clients (including society)

- can safely assume (rather than ensure as in a Mega needs assessment) that what it delivers to internal and societal clients adds value to them

- wants to ensure profitability in the short-term

- is engaged in a tactical planning process.

For example, if we had started at the Macro-level needs assessment for the BIC scenario described in chapter 3, rather than starting by defining an Ideal Vision, we would have started by looking at their current mission. The assumption—a risky assumption—would have been that BIC's mission is directly linked to customer needs and well-being, and is therefore already making a positive contribution to its customers and society.

Process for Conducting

As with all needs assessments, you will want to form a needs assessment team. The team should include representation from all groups who could either affect or be affected by the Macro-level needs assessment. This would include high-level executives, mid-level management, employees, and customers (see Figure 4.1).

Figure 4.1   Macro-Level Needs Assessment Process

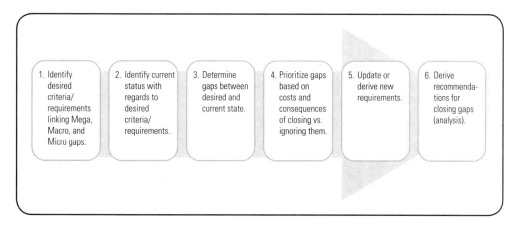

Step 1—Identify Macro Objectives, Indicators, and Targets

Macro objectives are usually defined by an organizational mission. However, these missions are not always stated in terms of results. Often, they include references to "being the best" or "using all our resources" or "trying hard" and other fuzzy phrases that say nothing about what the organization commits to deliver, or wants to accomplish. Part of your task is to "translate" these good intentions into measurable results the organization commits to deliver. Without clear results, there is little accountability and much inefficiency.

At this point, you will want to convene a meeting with your needs assessment and planning partners with the goal of defining, or clarifying, the organizational mission and the relevant indicators that help track its progress. For example, let's take the BIC mission objective from the previous chapter:

> By the end of fiscal year 2023, the Bewell Insurance Company will remain as leaders in the industry by demonstrating perfect customer health records. To accomplish our mission, we will reduce the incidence of avoidable diseases (each year until the ideal is reached) through at least a 13 percent increase in early cancer detection though early screening compliance among women of target age, and at least 21 percent among men of target age. We will also reduce heart, and other obesity-related disease by a reduction of at least 32 percent in the number of customers who are morbidly obese. We will also seek a reduction in drug abuse by increasing the number of successfully treated clients by at least 28 percent. BIC also commits to an increase of at least 20 percent in physical abuse screening for women as well as an increase of at least 32 percent in their successful recovery from physically abusive conditions. We will reduce the number of injuries suffered on the job by four per year until zero is reached. We will accomplish this in part by ensuring a safe work environment for our employees that will be evidenced by zero injuries in the workplace. We will consistently reduce adjudicated incidents of discrimination until the number reaches zero and remains at zero.

In this case, we know that the mission is already aligned to Mega, as we can see that it includes Ideal Vision and Vital Signs indicators (if your organizational mission is not linked to Mega, be sure to help your planning partners make that link, even if a formal Mega-level needs assessment will not be carried out at this point). In any case, there is also reference to "remain as leaders in the industry." But what does that mean? This is what has to be translated into a series of Macro-level results and indicators.

Facilitate a meeting with your needs assessment partners that helps them collectively agree on what results and indicators would provide evidence that BIC was indeed the industry leader. We recommend that you think carefully about what information would be required in order to have a productive meeting.

The product of this meeting might look something like what is illustrated in Table 4.1.

Table 4.1   Measurable Indicators for BIC's Mission Objective

Mission Element	Dimensions	Measurable Indicator
• Leader in industry	• Market domination	• Market share
	• Profitable	• Net profit • Net profit margin
	• Big revenue	• Gross revenue • Net revenue
	• Low expenses	• Fixed expenses • Variable expenses
	• Satisfied customers	• Customer satisfaction survey scores • Customer complaints

Once measurable indicators have been identified for the mission, the discussion should focus on targets. The needs assessment partners will likely require information to help them come up with appropriate targets; for example, industry standards, historical BIC performance data, and so on. However, since these indicators were just identified, it is possible that at this point, not all the necessary context is available to establish useful targets and another meeting might be required.

Be sure to remind everyone that setting high and challenging objectives based on the best industry standards (and perhaps beyond, if they are serious about being leaders) is a critical aspect of this step, providing them context and highlighting that final targets will come after data is collected about the organization's current status (What Is) with regards to the Macro objectives. Also keep in mind that unlike the Mega level, where the horizon will be long-term, Macro time horizons are shorter-term and tend to be in the one- to five-year range.

Step 2—Identify Current Status as It Relates to Organizational Mission

As with all needs assessments, this is the step where we collect data on What Is. Carefully consider the indicators you identified and select the most appropriate sources. These might include:

- market analyses
- stock market reported performance of your organization and others in the industry
- industry reports
- legislated standards
- strategic plans
- customer surveys and complaint records
- consulting reports.

As we mentioned in chapter 3, there may be a wealth of information right in your own organization. Be sure to check its availability before spending additional resources to collect the same data all over again.

Also, it is important to consider the appropriateness of the data collection instruments you will use in light of the type of data you will collect, as well as the source of that data. For instance, if you are looking for profit margins, do not include it as a question in some sort of internal survey questionnaire. Profit margin is hard data—independently verifiable—and will already be documented and tracked by the organization. All that would be required in that situation is a document review. (See Guerra-López, 2007; 2008 for more detailed guidance on data collection and analysis methodology).

For our BIC example, a sample piece of the final product of the data collection effort is illustrated in Table 4.2.

Table 4.2   Current Status of Macro Indicators as Compared to Desired Targets

Macro: What Should Be	Current Status: What Is
• At least 40% market share	• 30% market share
• At least 35% net profit margin	• 23% in net profit margin
• At least $950 million in gross revenue	• $790 million in gross revenue
• 100% customer satisfaction	• 92% customer satisfaction level from survey scores

Step 3—Determine Gaps Between Desired and Current State

In this step we articulate the precise gap between What Should Be and What Is at the Macro level. This is something that can be done as part of the analysis stage, prior to conducting a follow-up meeting with the entire Macro-level needs assessment and planning partners. Here, these measurable gaps will become the basis for formulating or updating specific organizational objectives, and later, in step 6, getting into the gap analysis, so that proper solutions, interventions, and other methods or means can be selected (see Table 4.3).

Now that the BIC needs assessment partners have identified real gaps in results based on actual data about valid indicators of our macro intentions, it is time to prioritize them.

Table 4.3   BIC Macro-Level Gaps

Ideal Vision: What Should Be	Current Status: What Is	Gap
• At least 40% market share	• 30% market share	• 10% market share
• At least 35% net profit margin	• 23% in net profit margin	• 12% net profit margin
• At least $950 million in gross revenue	• $790 million	• $160 million
• 100% customer satisfaction	• 92% customer satisfaction	• 8% in customer satisfaction levels

Step 4—Prioritize Gaps Based on Costs and Consequences of Closing vs. Ignoring Them

As we have previously discussed, not all gaps have the same sense of urgency, and it may not be feasible to address them all at the present time. The purpose of prioritizing them is to identify which are the most critical to address right now, which might guide our organizational plans for the next year or two. The needs assessment and planning partners will have to make the actual decision.

You will support those decisions through a facilitated discussion with needs assessment and planning partners based on the type of criteria we established for a Mega-level needs assessment. In fact these are relevant for any needs assessment, at any level:

- *Magnitude:* This refers to the size of the gap.

- *Costs and consequences:* The costs (financial and non-financial) of a gap might be greater than for others, even if their magnitude isn't as big as others.

- *Organizational resources and capital (financial and non-financial):* While not the criterion with the heaviest weight, the prioritization discussion should include some reference of this as a matter of context or climate.

Solicit other important criteria from needs assessment and planning partners that are particularly relevant to their organization. While you want to be open to their criteria, be sure to steer them toward results-oriented criteria rather than any focus on particular means and methods. As before, the following priority levels will be relevant:

- **High priority:** Carries large costs and consequences associated with ignoring the need at this point in time.

- **Moderate priority:** Carries some costs and consequences associated with ignoring the need at this point in time.

- **Low priority:** Carries minimal costs and consequences associated with ignoring the need at this or at a later time.

The end result of that prioritization session for BIC might look something like Table 4.4 and expanded on further in the BIC example that follows.

Table 4.4   Gaps and Their Levels of Priority

Gap	Priority Level
• 10% market share	• Medium
• 12% net profit margin	• High
• $160 million revenue	• Medium
• 8% customer satisfaction	• High

This costs-consequences data will assist management in allocation of resources for each need area. Detailed models for quantifying costs and consequences for planning (and during the evaluation phase) are available. One popular one is provided by Phillips (1997) for estimating return-on-investment (up through but not formally including Mega) and another developed by Bernardez (2005) that quantifies costs and consequences for the entire OEM.

BIC needs assessment partners decided one of the highest priorities for the organization is to increase their customer satisfaction score, as this was central to influencing other critical indicators. For example, they agreed that increased customer satisfaction would positively affect customer retention, which would also have an impact on their revenue, and perhaps even help the control costs spent on new customer acquisition, which is a more costly proposition than retaining current customers. There was also a high priority placed on addressing the net profit margin, as profitability was one of the original areas that the VP of human resources raised as an increasing concern. Focus on the net profit margin, they considered, would directly help the organization focus on efficiency. While they felt that increasing revenue and market share was important to the organization, they recognized that those would likely be a byproduct of focusing first and foremost on customer satisfaction.

The partners estimated the costs to ignore or not close the gaps in results as shown in Table 4.5.

Table 4.5   Gaps, Their Priority Levels, and Possible Risks

Gap	Priority Level	Possible Risk of Not Meeting
• 10% market share	• Medium	• Possible reduction of share value of 7%
• 12% net profit margin	• High	• Loss in share value and market share of 13%
• $160 million revenue	• Medium	• Possible reduction of share value of 4 to 6%
• 8% customer satisfaction	• High	• Loss of 12 at market share and reduction of 4 to 7% in share value. Also possible penalties of oversight agencies.

Step 5—Update Organizational Objectives

Once these priorities are established and agreed upon by the needs assessment partners, they should be stated in terms of specific objectives that are to be the key focus of the organization over the next year.

A careful analysis will now follow as the basis for establishing solution criteria, and finally selecting the best methods means to help the organization reach these key objectives.

> BIC's Macro-level objectives were stated as follows:
>
> - By the end of fiscal year 2013, BIC will improve their customer satisfaction as measured by at least an eight-point increase in customer satisfaction scores.
>
> - By the end of fiscal year 2013, BIC will see an increase in their net profit margin of at least 12 percent, as certified by an independent auditing report.

Step 6—Derive Recommendations for Closing Gaps (Analysis)

As previously mentioned in chapter 3, recommendations will stem from a series of analyses that help us understand why the performance gaps exist, and what criteria should be met in order to for a solution to successfully address those gaps. Chapter 7 provides a detailed description of each of these analyses and how to use them to make effective recommendations.

Challenges of Conducting a Macro-Level Needs Assessment

It is important to keep in mind that the organization exists in the context of a societal system. If the organization does not link its accomplishments to external requirements of value added to clients and society, its long-term health and survival may be compromised.

As with all needs assessment levels, it is always a challenge to get those partners who are eager to take action to start by documenting valid organizational needs and foci. What we would recommend is to highlight that starting with a needs assessment is taking immediate action, and ensures that future actions are well guided and supported.

All needs assessments have the same characteristics of identifying and documenting results gaps between What Is and What Should Be. The different levels of needs assessments focus on one of the three levels of the OEM and must be linked and aligned with Mega if organizational success is to be designed and delivered.

Chapter Summary

This chapter presented a holistic approach to a Macro-level needs assessment, including why and when one should be conducted. We also discussed a step-by-step process for how to conduct a Macro-level needs assessment, which also included guidance on how to update objectives using data from a Macro-level needs assessment.

Chapter 5
Performing a Micro-Level Needs Assessment

What's in This Chapter?

- What is a Micro-level needs assessment

- How and when to perform a Micro-level assessment

- Overcoming the challenges of conducting a Micro-level assessment

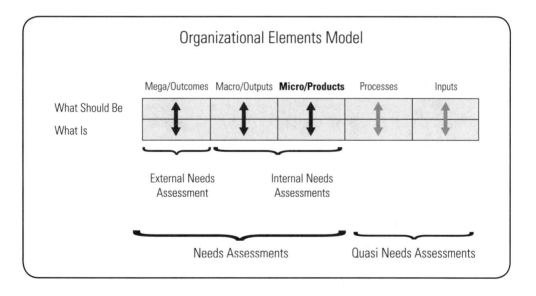

This chapter provides a third type of needs assessment: one that assumes that needs identified and closed at this level will add value to organizational contributions as well as make societal contributions.

First, you should understand the concept of conducting Micro-level needs assessment in the context of the Organizational Elements Model. Again, we will use the BIC case study as starting point:

> *The new legislative changes in the healthcare industry also have implications for BIC's sales and service professionals. They will be required to be more competent in many aspects of the business and also deal with a whole new set of job requirements, while maintaining and growing key relationships. Burnout of the sales force tends to take place after only a few years on the job, and with higher expectations, the burnout rate is expected to accelerate.*
>
> *BIC's chief learning officer has just contacted you to help ensure the competence of sales and service professionals, including updating job requirements, in the face of all the changes.*
>
> *What do you do?*

What Is a Micro-Level Needs Assessment?

A Micro-level needs assessment is a process for identifying and prioritizing gaps between desired results versus current results at the individual, group, or department performance level. Essentially, these results are the building-block objectives that when taken together, help the organization reach its Macro results and, in turn, help the organization deliver on its Mega contributions.

Relevant accomplishments at this level tend to be around those that relate to specific performer deliverables, for example, successfully completed service calls, successfully repaired automobiles, or sales executed. For a healthcare organization, this might include things like recertified professionals, evaluations completed, average length of stay, and maintained bed occupancy. For an educational institution, relevant results might relate to student test scores in specific subject areas, teacher certification or recertification, student attendance, student referrals, and so on.

It is important to note that there might be various levels of Micro, or operational, results that work in hierarchies and networks, to equal one or more Macro-level results. We suggest that you carefully identify these value chains, so that the Micro-level needs assessment looks at all relevant levels of Micro results. The BIC case study will be continued in this chapter to illustrate Micro-level results that are linked to Macro and Mega.

Likewise, you should carefully consider the link of the Micro-level results that will be the subject of your Micro needs assessment, to the relevant Macro- and Mega-level results, even if conducting formal Macro- and Micro-level needs assessments are beyond the scope of your needs assessment.

We can't stress enough how important it is to check the value of what you are doing to the organization's effectiveness and its contributions to external customers and society. The reason behind this urging is to save you from well-intention failure that can occur. According to Deming and Juran (Deming, 1972; 1986; 1990; Juran, 1988), 80 to 90 percent of all performance breakdowns are not from problems at the individual or small group (Micro) level but dysfunction at the Macro and even Mega levels. And not only can failure come from addressing needs at the inappropriate level, it can also be caused by starting at the process level by such tools as a "training needs assessment" that usually assumes that training is required. Eighty to 90 percent probability of failure is a very high risk.

Conducting a rigorous Micro-level needs assessment can ensure the right focus on the right performers and performance. This in turn will help you align the right performance support solutions and initiatives—such as training or professional development, incentive programs, technology tools—with what your organization uses, does, produces, delivers, and the value added to external clients.

While a Micro-level needs assessment can help us ensure operational effectiveness, we reiterate that only a Mega-level needs assessment can help you ensure strategic effectiveness.

When to Use a Micro-Level Needs Assessment

You should use a Micro-level needs assessment when your organization finds itself in any of the following scenarios:

- recognizes that what the organizations uses, does, and produces should be aligned with and add value to internal stakeholders

- assumes (rather than ensures) that what is produced adds value to the organization and beyond

- introduces changes that will have on impact on job requirements and improved performance

- is experiencing challenging symptoms related to particular jobs or performers
- is engaged in operational planning.

Process for Conducting

Your needs assessment team should include representation from all groups who could either affect or be affected by the Micro-level needs assessment. This might include mid-level management, supervisors, employees, and customers that affect or are affected by the particular performance (or performance objective) in question. You will also want to secure commitment from them to help you obtain full access to the data you will require (see Figure 5.1).

Figure 5.1   Micro-Level Needs Assessment Process

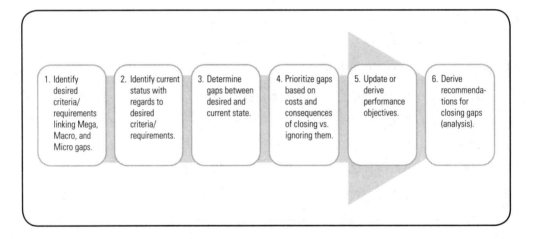

Step 1—Identify Performance Objectives, Indicators, and Targets and Alignment to Mega

Performance objectives indicate the required performance and standards of an individual or group of performers. As with Mega and Macro levels, objectives are always about accomplishments, not about "how" we do something. For example, objectives for our BIC sales and service professionals might look like those listed in the sidebar. Required performance should always be defined in terms of specific, observable, and measurable results. Your needs assessment team will provide a good source of initial information. Managers and supervisors should help you clarify what exact performance objectives are required (best based on needs data), as well as human resource records, external industry standards, and even your top performers (for the performance in question). You may get some of this information through a group meeting, or you may require individual meetings.

> - *Sales and service professionals acquire at least 20 new accounts per quarter.*
> - *Sales and service professionals retain at least 98 percent of current accounts at all times.*
> - *Sales and service professionals acquire at least 20 new accounts per quarter.*
> - *Sales and service professionals retain at least 98 percent of current accounts at all times.*
> - *All sales and service professionals meet or exceed their individualized monthly sales goals.*
> - *All sales and service professionals demonstrate competence with new group membership rules, as demonstrated by acquiring new industry certification.*
> - *All sales and service professionals achieve an overall average score of at least 4.5 on the 5-point scale customer satisfaction survey.*

If you are conducting the needs assessment because a performance problem has been detected, or at least symptoms of a performance problem, then those who initially perceived the problem will be a primary source of information. Ask questions such as:

- Why do they believe there is a problem?
- What evidence has led them to this conclusion?
- What performance objectives are relevant to the perceived problem?
- What individuals or groups are being affected?

In the case of BIC, in addition to clarifying performance requirements that will ensure sales and service professional competence, there is also an expressed concern about burnout rate. This warrants a discussion with needs assessment partners about what constitutes "burnout," what indicators are used to measure burnout and what is a desired, or acceptable, level. You will get into the *why* of the burnout rate in step 6, when a series of analyses are conducted in order to make recommendations about how to close the gaps.

Your efforts to identify desired performance objectives may render both the desired accomplishment and the measurable criteria and target from the outset, or you may have to provide additional support in terms of helping your needs assessment partners come up with more precise and measurable criteria in order to clarify desired performance.

It is possible that a significant change warrants that altogether new performance objectives are derived. It is also possible that no significant change has necessarily occurred, but rather that there is some suspected discrepancy in performance. Remember, this is not the time to get into detailed analysis or discussions around *why*, rather, this is the time to clarify *what* performance is required.

The specific performance objectives you come up with during this process may or may not be exactly what has been used previously as desired performance. However, what you come up with now should certainly reflect what you wish desired performance to be from this point forward, as this will become the basis for identifying gaps, and subsequently, the best solution set. For this reason, we can't emphasize enough how important it is to *obtain full consensus* from the needs assessment partners on what the desired performance objectives should and will be.

Table 5.1 presents an example of how you may depict the specific indicators to be measured, for each of the performance objectives relevant to your Micro-level needs assessment.

Table 5.1   Performance Objectives and Specific Indicators

Performance Objectives	Specific Indicators
• Sales and service professionals acquire at least 20 new accounts per quarter.	• Number of new accounts acquired per quarter
• Sales and service professionals retain at least 95% of current accounts at all times.	• Percent of current active accounts
• All sales and service professionals meet or exceed their individualized monthly sales goals.	• Sales dollars • Sales volume
• All sales and service professionals demonstrate competence with new group membership rules, as demonstrated by acquiring new industry certification.	• Sales and service professional certification status • Customer satisfaction scores
• All sales and service professional achieve an overall average score of at least 4.5 on the 5-point scale customer satisfaction survey.	• Employee satisfaction scores • Employee feedback from mentor coaching sessions

Step 2—Identify Current Status as Related to Your Performance Objectives

As with before, much of the data collection occurs here, with the essential goal of identifying the current status of human performance with regards to the performance objectives identified in the previous step.

Data collection is usually conducted by the needs assessors, with the help of some of the needs assessment partners who committed to providing access to the necessary information. Their commitment will be very useful in ensuring data collection goes as planned, as issues of access to data can significantly hinder progress of the needs assessment process.

You would first look at the measurable indicators that were previously identified and collect the appropriate data from the appropriate sources, through the appropriate data collection methods and instruments.

One of the methods commonly used in this step are observations of typical performers (to be compared with top performers), or another standard agreed upon during step 1. You can also review current records that document the current levels of a given indicator. For example, sales reports would likely reveal sales dollars and sales volumes of the performers in question, while a review of current customer satisfaction survey results would be warranted to learn about their scores. If you were looking at more specific indicators that warranted direct observation of performers, then you would likely want to develop a customized behavioral observation protocol to help collect data on frequency and quality of the target behaviors.

An overview of methodological considerations is provided in chapter 8. Guerra-López (2008) provides concrete information on data collection and analysis methodology.

The final product of this step might be illustrated as shown in Table 5.2 below.

Table 5.2   Side-by-Side Comparison of What Should Be vs. What Is

Desired Performance: What Should Be	Current Status: What Is
• At least 20 new accounts acquired per quarter	• 10 new accounts acquired per quarter
• At least 95% current active accounts	• 78% current active accounts
• At least $500,000 in sales per month • At least 25 units sold per month	• $350,000 in sales per month • 16 units sold per month
• 100% sales and service professionals achieve certification	• 90% sales and service professionals achieving professional certification
• Average score of at least 4.5 out of 5 in customer satisfaction	• Average score in customer satisfaction is 3.5
• Average satisfaction scores of at least 4.5 in quarterly employee satisfaction surveys throughout the year	• Average sales and service professional satisfaction scores are 3

Step 3—Determine the Gaps Between Desired and Current States

In this step, you list the full range of gaps between current and desired states. These specific gaps will become the basis for the new or updated performance objectives, after they are prioritized.

You should derive this full list as an input for the prioritization meeting with needs assessment and planning partners (step 4). That list is illustrated as what is shown in Table 5.3.

Table 5.3   The Gaps Between What Should Be and What Is

Desired Performance: What Should Be	Current Status: What Is	Gap
• At least 20 new accounts acquired per quarter	• 10 new accounts acquired per quarter	• 10 new accounts per quarter
• At least 95% current active accounts	• 78% current active accounts	• 17% in current active accounts
• At least $500,000 in sales per month • 25 units sold per month	• 350,000 in sales per month • 16 units sold per month	• $150,000 in sales per month • 9 units per month
• 100% sales and service professionals achieve certification	• 90% sales and service professionals achieving professional certification	• 10% in professional certification
• Average score of at least 4.5 out of 5 in customer satisfaction	• Average score in customer satisfaction is 3.5	• 1 point in customer satisfaction scores
• Average score of at least 4.5 out 5 in employee satisfaction	• Average score in employee satisfaction is 3	• 1.5 points in employee satisfaction scores

Step 4—Prioritize Gaps Based on Costs and Consequences of Closing vs. Ignoring Them

Prioritizing gaps is always part of a needs assessment. While all gaps are likely to be important, there will be different levels of importance that help the needs assessment partners determine what will be the focus of immediate action, and what will be addressed at a later time. At this point, you will want to set up a prioritization meeting with the needs assessment and planning partners so that they can make those decisions. As the needs assessor, your efforts are focused on supporting their decision-making process, rather than making the decision yourself.

As before, one of the ways of supporting your partners' decision-making process is by sharing some options in terms of priority levels.

• *Magnitude:* This essentially determines the size of the gap.

- *Costs and consequences:* The costs (financial and non-financial) of a gap might be greater than for others, even if their magnitude isn't as big as others. Two levels of costs and consequences might relate to Macro and Mega impact. For example, if a given performance gap has significant potential impact over Macro objectives and strategic aims, then even if relatively small in magnitude, ignoring it could carry a significant cost and negative consequences. Chapter 5 provides additional guidance on costs-consequences assessment models that will be useful here.

- *Organizational resources and capital (financial and non-financial):* While not the criterion with the heaviest weight, the prioritization discussion should include some reference to this as a matter of context or climate.

These are some suggestions, and in our experience, most categories of prioritization criteria fall under one of these. Still, it is helpful to the needs assessment partners' buy-in process for you to be open to their suggestions. If you see that their additional suggestions fall under one of these categories, explain how their suggestions are a good example of one of these categories. It is always useful to see their ideas reflected in the work that is being conducted.

As before, the following priority levels will be relevant:

- **High priority:** Carries large costs and consequences associated with ignoring the need at this point in time.

- **Moderate priority:** Carries some costs and consequences associated with ignoring the need at this point in time.

- **Low priority:** Carries minimal costs and consequences associated with ignoring the need at this or at a later time.

The end result of that prioritization session for BIC might look something like Table 5.4 and as further illustrated in the BIC example that follows.

Table 5.4   Gaps and Priority Levels

Gap	Priority Level
• At least 10 new accounts per quarter	• Medium
• At least 17% in current active accounts	• High
• At least $150,000 in sales per month • 9 units per month	• High
• At least 10% in professional certification	• High
• At least 1 point in customer satisfaction scores	• High
• At least 1.5 points in employee satisfaction scores	• High

BIC's needs assessment and planning partners decided focusing on retaining active accounts through increased customer satisfaction was absolutely critical to their Macro- and Mega-level objectives. This was made apparent through the discussion around costs and consequences of ignoring these particular gaps. It also seemed to them that if they placed high priority focus on satisfying customers and retaining them, this would have natural implications for monthly sales, so potentially, they could leverage a solution set (when they get to the methods-means analysis) that could impact these multiple indicators.

Another high priority area that became quite "obvious," as one of the needs assessment partners said it, was the job satisfaction of sales and service professionals. If they don't find satisfaction in their work, feel undervalued, and lose motivation to stay in their position (or even in the organization), any other solutions implemented to support their performance will be useless, as they will not have any stake in the success of those solutions, the department, or the organization.

Additionally, they have direct contact with customers, and therefore, have the potential to considerably affect Mega- and Macro-level objectives. Moreover, the cost of hiring, training, and getting new sales and service professionals to a top-performer level represents a significantly higher cost than to provide the support required to maintain a high level of satisfaction with the job. Therefore, the needs assessment partners felt that in order for the department and organization to thrive, maintaining sales and service professionals' satisfaction was key.

Finally, they decided that while new account acquisition is certainly important for their position, they would have to wait for the new marketing and customer acquisition strategy that was being launched as an organization-wide initiative at the request of BIC's VP, in response to the new legislation. Once that was defined, they could proceed to establish relevant performance requirements for the sales and service professionals.

Step 5—Update Performance Objectives

The precise performance objectives that will become the target, not only of sales and service professionals at BIC, but also of the solution set that will be selected through the analysis process (step 6), are as follows:

- Sales and service professionals will increase their current active accounts by at least 17 percent over the next calendar year.

- Sales and service professionals will increase their sales figures by at least $150,000 per month; and increase units sold by nine units per month over the next calendar year.

- Sales and service professionals professionally certified will increase by at least 10 percent over the next calendar year.

- Sales and service professionals will increase their customer satisfaction scores by 1 point within the next three months, and maintain a 4.5 average at all times thereafter.

Stating the objectives in this way will help ensure clear responsibilities and accountabilities, once recommendations are made (step 6).

Step 6—Make Recommendations for Closing Gaps (Analysis)

Only a causal analysis will enable us to identify the source of performance discrepancies or gaps, such as inconsistent performance specifications, lack of positive consequences for expected behavior, lack of required skills and knowledge to reach performance objectives, and others. Refer to chapter 7 for an in-depth look at causal analysis, and other analysis tools that will help you recommend the most useful set of solutions.

Challenges of Conducting a Micro-Level Needs Assessment

As with all levels of needs assessments, getting buy-in from all needs assessment partners is critical, and not always straightforward. There could be many competing responsibilities that are vying for your partners' attention, and the needs assessment may not always make it to the top of the list. Be understanding of this, but also be consistent in keeping them informed, and holding them accountable for their contributions to the needs assessment. It is also vital that the group understands and commits to adding value at the Macro and Micro levels to avoid failure.

Access to data can be a challenge as well. While you would expect access to data to be relatively straightforward, since the data is being sought to improve organizational performance, people can be very wary of granting access to data that they fear might reflect on them negatively. Ensure that you gain the trust of those who have, or will help you access, the data. Assuring anonymity, whenever possible, can go a long way in helping people feel comfortable with sharing information.

Chapter Summary

This chapter defined a Micro-level needs assessment and described when and how to perform one, and the related risks of using this level as a starting point. A Micro-level needs assessment has the same characteristics as any needs assessment. It identifies valid gaps in results between What Is and What Should Be so that those needs may be placed in priority order based on the costs to meet the needs as compared to the costs to ignore the needs. This level of needs assessment focuses on individual and small group performance and contributions, while linking them to results and contributions at the Macro and Mega levels.

Chapter 6
Performing a Quasi Needs Assessment

What's in This Chapter?

- What is a Quasi needs assessment and when to use it

- How to identify and prioritize valid performance criteria and show valid gaps

- Updating and developing new criteria and making recommendations

- Dealing with typical challenges

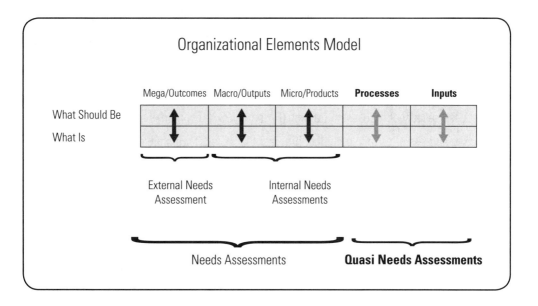

Organizational Elements Model

In literature and in conventional practice, tools such as "training needs assessment" are popular, but starting with one can lead to disappointing results. This is not because the techniques are not valuable, but because they start with means and not ends. Training can, if designed and justified correctly, be a vital and important part of any organization's effectiveness. However, training should not be designed and initiated without first ensuring that doing so will meet important needs.

First, let's put Quasi needs assessments in the organizational context. Again, let's consider the case of BIC. Rather than getting a request that focuses on the competence and performance requirements for sales and service professionals, the learning and development manager's request deals specifically with how to enhance the current training, so that content related to the new legislative requirements could be added to current training, without increasing training time and other training-related costs. One of the ideas that she is currently considering is increasing online training capabilities, and reducing traditional face-to-face classroom training.

Given this background, how do you proceed?

What Is a Quasi Needs Assessment?

A Quasi needs assessment is a process used to identify gaps in methods and means, such as training or organizational development. For example, knowledge is a means to human competence, therefore a Quasi needs assessment of knowledge would entail looking at the gaps between What Should Be known (as opposed to accomplished) and What Is currently known by performers on a specific topic.

Rossett's Training Needs Assessment (TNA) is a prime example of a Quasi needs assessment process because it focuses on training (Rossett, 1987). Training is a means, a specific solution used to address gaps in knowledge, if in fact that is what we should do in order to improve performance (something we would only know if we had done a needs assessment at a Micro level, at a minimum).

Mager and Pipe (1999) further distinguish among various types of knowledge gaps, cautioning us to consider that not all knowledge gaps require training; some might be well addressed through additional information, a job aid, or other more cost-effective solutions. This point will be further explored in the next chapter, when we discuss various analysis tools that help us identify solution requirements before jumping into solution selection.

Variations of a *process improvement* approach could also be considered a Quasi needs assessment. For example, one approach often taken to improve a process is to begin with an articulation of the process goal and deliverable, and then depict the ideal process flow.

Subsequently, the current process is depicted and gaps are identified for resolution. As you will see later in this chapter, this process improvement approach resembles the Quasi needs assessment process.

Instructional, Learner, and Context Analysis

Instructional, learner, and context analysis, and other front-end tasks that are often associated with needs assessments, are more specific examples of Quasi needs assessments, particularly if you consider that these are specific tasks often carried out in the contexts of training needs assessments. We define these as *Quasi needs assessments* because, while they deal with gaps, the gaps are related to means (such as training) and resources (Inputs) and must be rationally or explicitly linked to needs assessments at the Mega, Macro, and Micro levels.

A Quasi needs assessment can also be used to identify gaps in resources, perhaps in a resource planning process. For example, a Quasi needs assessment of training facilities could be used to determine the gaps between the number of training facilities and the required capabilities they should possess in order to accommodate the training function.

A Quasi needs assessment of performance support tools, for example, could be conducted to identify gaps between the specific tools performers should have to be able to carry out their work, versus what they currently use. Again, the assumption is that the tools considered to be required for the job are actually tied to a desired set of accomplishments. This assumption could only be confirmed through a needs assessment—at the Mega, Macro, and Micro levels.

In summary, while a Micro-level needs assessment can ensure you focus on real performance gaps, which in turn will help you align the right performance support solutions and initiatives, a Quasi needs assessment can help ensure the efficiency of these methods and means. It will not ensure effectiveness. Ensuring operational effectiveness begins with a Micro-level needs assessment, while strategic effectiveness will only be ensured through a Mega-level needs assessment.

When to Use a Quasi Needs Assessment

A Quasi-level needs assessment is most appropriate when your organization:

- recognizes that what the organization uses and does should be aligned

- assumes (rather than ensures) that what is used and done within the organization adds value to internal stakeholders and beyond

- is experiencing challenges related to processes or resources

- is about to implement a new process or resource

- is engaged in resource planning.

Process for Conducting

Once again, one the most important elements to coordinate from the outset is to identify your partners. You will want to form a Quasi needs assessment and planning team that will help review, provide feedback, approve, and in some cases, directly participate in the technical aspects of the process, such as data collection, or at the very least, help you gain access to the required data.

Your team could include the relevant manager(s), supervisor(s), employees, customers, and anyone else who might affect or be affected by the process or resource that is the basis of this Quasi needs assessment.

The Quasi needs assessment process is illustrated in Figure 6.1.

Figure 6.1 The Quasi Needs Assessment Process

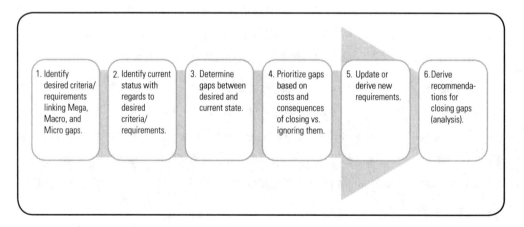

1. Identify desired criteria/ requirements linking Mega, Macro, and Micro gaps.

2. Identify current status with regards to desired criteria/ requirements.

3. Determine gaps between desired and current state.

4. Prioritize gaps based on costs and consequences of closing vs. ignoring them.

5. Update or derive new requirements.

6. Derive recommenda- tions for closing gaps (analysis).

Step 1—Identify Desired Criteria/Requirements

One of the commonalities between a Quasi needs assessment and the ones described for the Mega, Macro, and Micro levels is that the starting point is always defining What Should Be. In this case, you and the Quasi needs assessment partners want to clarify the process or resource that you would like to optimize, and specify what the ideal criteria for that process or resource should be. This What Should Be will be the basis for the identification of Quasi needs or gaps.

A facilitated discussion with the needs assessment partners is perhaps the best vehicle for the identification of the desired criteria. It is critical that all partners participate and agree on the desired criteria, as this will not only be the foundation for the rest of the Quasi needs assessment process, but also the implemented recommendations that will follow.

One of the very critical aspects of this discussion should include the alignment of the target process or input to Micro, Macro, and Mega level needs. If you (or some other group in the organization) have already conducted needs assessments at those levels, and improving this process of input was essentially one of the recommendations that stemmed out of those efforts, you are starting with solid ground. The chances that improving this process or input will not only improve efficiencies, but also contribute toward effectiveness, is pretty strong.

If, however, needs assessments at these other levels have not been conducted, yet you are nonetheless tasked with carrying out the Quasi-level needs assessment, you will want to, at the very least, take advantage of this discussion to gain formal input and consensus from your partners about which Micro, Macro, and Mega level objectives this process or input is linked to. It is important that they take ownership of those linkages; therefore, we recommend that you act as a facilitator, rather than a decision maker. This helps ensure accountability is well placed for the success of this Quasi-level needs assessment, and perhaps, helps decision makers reconsider starting at this level, if no results-driven needs assessments have been previously conducted.

In our BIC scenario, these specifications might include those listed in the sidebar on the following page.

Step 2—Identify Current Status as It Relates to Desired Criteria and Requirements

With the required specifications now defined, you have a good sense of what data sources will be useful in gathering data about the current status of those specifications. As with other types of needs assessments, be sure to consider the type of data you are interested in prior to selecting any preferred data collection approaches. Also, be prepared to consider a variety of sources for the information.

For example, if we want to ensure we meet the criterion: *"Sales and service professionals' satisfaction with training should not suffer, as indicated by training evaluations,"* we may not

- *Training must cover all new legislation-related changes relevant to sales and service professionals' jobs.*

- *Training must not eliminate any current content that is central to sales and service professionals' jobs; however, obsolete content areas may be eliminated.*

- *Training time must not be higher than that required for current training.*

- *Training should be enhanced or supported with the use of on-the-job guides.*

- *Training must not add any significant costs for a sustained period of time. (Significant is defined as anything greater than 10 percent for an initial period of two years. Thereafter, costs should be expected to decrease by at least 20 percent.)*

- *Sales and service professionals should be able to access the training at their convenience, during provided windows of time during work hours, without any travel or any additional costs incurred.*

- *Training capabilities should be enhanced by taking advantage of our in-house, state-of-the-art technology resources (including networked computers; online learning platforms; modern training facilities, and anything else we currently have at our disposal).*

- *Sales and service professionals' satisfaction with training should not suffer, as indicated by training evaluations.*

only want to look at past training evaluation findings to review current satisfaction with training, but we may also want to ask sales and service professionals directly (perhaps through focus groups, interviews, or any other data collection methods that are appropriate for the situation). One way of leveraging this data collection effort is to also ask about what aspects are most important for them, how their satisfaction could be ensured (within the guidelines provided in step 1), and what other general suggestions they may have.

While the perspective of sales and service professionals should be represented by at least one member serving as a Quasi needs assessment partner, getting their input through this other approach could go a long way. Table 6.1 illustrates how the final product of step 2 may be illustrated.

Table 6.1   Current Status as Compared to Desired Criteria

Desired Criteria: What Should Be	Current Status: What Is
• Training must cover all new legislation-related changes relevant to sales and service professionals' jobs.	• None of the current training reflects the legislative changes.
• Training must not eliminate any current content that is central to sales and service professionals' jobs, however, obsolete content areas may be eliminated.	• Of the training modules, eight out of 15 across the four learning programs available for sales and service professionals include at least one learning objective that has become obsolete as a result of the legislative changes.
• Training time must not be higher than that required for current training.	• Three of the four current training programs for sales and service professionals require 12 hours each, while one requires eight hours, for a total 44 hours.
• Training should be enhanced or supported with the use of on-the-job guides.	• There are only two job aids and sales and service professionals report they do not support performance, nor are they consistent with what they learned in training.
• Training must not add any significant costs for a sustained period of time. (Significant is defined as anything greater than 10% for an initial period of two years. Thereafter, costs should be expected to decrease by at least 20%.)	• Average cost for training development per program: $500,000. • Average cost for training facilitation per program per cohort: $115,000.
• Sales and service professionals should be able to access the training at their convenience, during provided windows of time during work hours, without any travel or any additional costs incurred.	• Sales and service professionals currently have to physically attend training when it is available. Availability is determined by training plans based on department capabilities rather than convenience for trainees. This causes some to miss training, and sometimes wait a year to be able to take it again.
• Training capabilities should be enhanced by taking advantage of our in-house state-of-the-art technology resources (e.g. networked computers; online learning platforms; modern training facilities, and anything else we currently have at our disposal).	• BIC has very extensive and sophisticated technology resources used for other purposes but they are not leveraged by training. There is only one pilot module for one of the training programs that is offered online, and there is low completion compliance for it.
• Sales and service professionals' satisfaction with training should not suffer, as indicated by training evaluations.	• Trainees are dissatisfied with current delivery approach and some of the content, including the mandate to take all modules of all programs, even when not directly relevant for their customer groups. They are also dissatisfied with current training scheduling.

Step 3—Determine Gaps Between the Desired and Current State

In this step, you clarify the specific gaps for your Quasi needs assessment partners, so that a discussion of their prioritization (step 4), can be facilitated. You and your technical team will likely want to prepare this table prior to that discussion, as a summary of all the data collection and analysis you carried out during steps 2 and 3.

Table 6.2 illustrates how gaps may be summarized and presented to stakeholders.

Table 6.2 Quasi Gaps or Quasi Needs

Desired Criteria: What Should Be	Current Status: What Is	Gap
• Training must cover all new legislation-related changes relevant to sales and service professionals' jobs.	• None of the four current training programs reflects the legislative changes, specifically.	• All four training programs will have to be revised to reflect legislative changes.
• Training must not eliminate any current content that is central to sales and service professionals' jobs, however, obsolete content areas may be eliminated.	• Seven out of the 15 training modules across the four learning programs available for sales and service professionals remain current and effective, even with the legislative changes.	• Eight out of the 15 training modules across the four learning programs include at least one learning objective that has become obsolete as a result of the legislative changes.
• New training time must not be higher than that required for current training.	• Three of the four current training programs for sales and service professionals require 12 hours each, while one requires eight hours, for a total 44 hours.	• No gap identified yet, but training updates will not exceed these times.
• Training should be enhanced or supported with the use of on-the-job guides.	• There are only two job aids and sales and service professionals report that they do not support performance, nor are they consistent with what they learned in training.	• Relevant job aids will be developed for each of the training programs, as required, once training is updated.
• Training must not add any significant costs for a sustained period of time (significant is defined as anything greater than 10% for an initial period of two years. Thereafter, costs should be expected to decrease by at least 20%).	• Average cost for training development per program: $500,000 • Average cost for training facilitation per program per cohort: $115,000	• No gap identified yet, but training costs will be within these guideless.
• Sales and service professionals should be able to access the training at their convenience, during provided windows of time during work hours, without any travel or any additional costs incurred.	• Sales and service professionals currently have to physically attend training when it is available. Availability is determined by training plans based on department capabilities rather than convenience for trainees. This causes some to miss training, and sometimes wait a year to be able to take it again.	• All training delivery options will conform to the new criteria.
• Training capabilities should be enhanced by taking advantage of our in-house state-of-the-art technology resources (e.g. networked computers; online learning platforms; modern training facilities, and anything else we currently have at our disposal).	• BIC has very extensive and sophisticated technology resources used for other purposes but they are not leveraged by training. There is only one pilot module for one of the training programs that is offered online, and there is low completion compliance for it.	• All BIC-owned technology will become multifunctional, and leveraged by training to enhance training delivery and satisfaction.
• Sales and service professionals' satisfaction with training should not suffer, as indicated by training evaluations.	• Trainees are dissatisfied with current delivery approach and some of the content, including the mandate to take all modules of all programs, even when not directly relevant for their customer groups. Also dissatisfied with current training scheduling.	• All training content will be rated as very useful by sales and service professionals as indicated by training evaluations. • Service and sales professionals will be very satisfied with new training scheduling and availability as indicated by training evaluations.

Step 4—Prioritize Gaps Based on Costs and Consequences of Closing vs. Ignoring Them

At this time, you will want convene another meeting with your Quasi needs assessment partners in order to present the gaps you have identified, as well as facilitate a discussion around placing the identified gaps in priority order.

As always, there are various categories of factors that will help them make a decision about how to best prioritize these needs (see step 4 in chapters 3, 4, and 5). These include gap magnitude, costs and consequences of closing a gap versus ignoring it, and the organizational resources required to close the gap. Remember to solicit additional prioritization criteria from your partners, so that they are even more vested in the process; and if you see that their additional suggestions fall under one of these categories, explain how their suggestions are a good example of one of these categories. It is always useful to see their ideas reflected in the work that is being conducted.

One of the most important considerations of costs and consequences is probably around how integral is that particular gap to accomplishing results at the Micro, Macro, and/or Mega levels. For example, the fact that none of the current training materials reflect the new legislative changes carries a significant cost and consequence at the Micro, Macro, and Mega levels. Being compliant with the law has a direct impact on the survival of BIC, as it could not only encounter a loss of current customers but also of potentially new ones, and it makes itself vulnerable to breaking the law and being sued, fined, and/or potentially closed down.

As before, defining clear levels of priority is critical for a transparent process and reaching consensus. A suggestion is:

- **High priority:** Carries large costs and consequences associated with ignoring the need at this point in time.

- **Moderate priority:** Carries some costs and consequences associated with ignoring the need at this point in time.

- **Low priority:** Carries minimal costs and consequences associated with ignoring the need at this or at a later time.

The end result of that prioritization session for BIC appears in Table 6.3.

Table 6.3   Prioritized Quasi Needs

Gap	Priority
• All four training programs will have to be revised to include legislative changes.	• High
• Eight out of the 15 training modules across the four learning programs include at least one learning objective that has become obsolete as a result of the legislative changes.	• High
• No gap identified yet, but training updates will not exceed these times.	• Medium
• Relevant job aids will be developed for each of the training programs, as required, once training is updated.	• Medium
• No gap identified yet, but training costs will be within these guideless.	• Medium
• All training delivery options will conform to the new criteria.	• High
• All BIC-owned technology will become multifunctional, and leveraged by training to enhance training delivery and satisfaction.	• Medium
• All training content will be rated as very useful by sales and service professionals as indicated by training evaluations. • Service and sales professionals will be very satisfied with new training scheduling and availability as indicated by training evaluations.	• High

In the BIC example the discussion of the Quasi needs assessment partners helped clarify that ensuring all training materials reflected the law was top priority. This includes both adding new content and removing obsolete content.

Further, there was a heated discussion around costs. It was ultimately considered of top priority to get this done within budget restrictions, since the current economic realities has forced training budgets (as well as others in the organization) to be significantly reduced. While the learning and development manager made her case to upper management that updating training to conform to new legislative requirements presented a significant additional cost to training operations, upper management saw this as an opportunity to revamp the sales and service training to make it leaner and more efficient. Therefore, only a temporary and modest increase (the initial two years) was approved, under the condition that training would become more efficient (as illustrated by a 20 percent savings thereafter); hence, the reason for this criteria being identified during step 1.

Leveraging current BIC technology requirements might help to this end, but it will not be considered of highest importance at this point, unless there it can be accomplished with relative ease and convenience or it ends up significantly helping control costs.

Also, maintaining sales and service professional satisfaction with training will be a high priority because of the already high burnout rate. The learning and development manager stressed that upper management had identified maintaining overall job satisfaction of sales and service professionals as a high priority for the organization, and wanted to ensure that training was seen as a driver rather than a barrier to this end. Improving training availability relates to satisfaction, as evidenced by feedback from sales and service professionals, therefore it was also considered a high priority gap.

Finally, all other criteria for which no formal gap had yet been identified—but that were important considerations—would continue to provide general guidance to future efforts, even if they had not been formally identified as top priority at this time.

Step 5—Update or Derive New Requirements

In this step, you formally update or derive new requirements, which will guide the selection of specific methods-means, and all subsequent focus of work for the training department team in charge of this initiative.

In the BIC example, priority requirements for the Legislative Compliance Training Team are listed in the sidebar below.

- *All four training programs will have to be revised to include legislative changes, including addition of new content and elimination of obsolete content, and meet measurable performance criteria.*

- *Sales and service professionals will indicate high satisfaction—at least 4.0 on a 5-point scale)—with training availability and scheduling.*

- *Sales and service professionals will indicate high satisfaction—at least 4.0 on a 5-point scale—of updated training.*

Step 6—Derive Recommendations

While a Quasi needs assessment is focused on means, improving these means will in turn depend on you selecting other means to close gaps between desired and current state. In the next chapter, we provide an in-depth discussion of a number of analysis tools that will help you ensure you select the right solutions.

Challenges of Conducting a Quasi Needs Assessment

One of the challenges of conducting a Quasi needs assessment is ensuring that improving the "how," or organizational processes and inputs, will ultimately add value to human and organizational performance. As we have discussed throughout this book, this is a big assumption, and the best way to ensure that improving methods and means will add value is by first conducing a results-driven needs assessment (see chapters 3, 4, and 5).

Another challenge is helping shape the mindsets of your Quasi needs assessment partners in such a way that other alternatives are considered, beyond what they are considering to "fix" or improve. That is always one of the biggest challenges of starting with means, rather than ends…the minute we focus on one solution, we have essentially eliminated all other—potentially better—options. One way to counter this challenge is to provide alternatives that meet the same criteria that were identified as critical during step 1 of the Quasi needs assessment process. If Quasi needs assessment partners are able to see that other options meet the criteria that are important to them, and can potentially do it cheaper, better, and faster, then there is a good chance that they will be open to at least considering these other options.

Chapter Summary

This chapter defined a Quasi needs assessment, and distinguished it from a needs assessment at the Mega, Macro, and Micro levels. We also provided guidance on when to use it, and how to identify and prioritize valid performance criteria and related gaps. Means, including training or human resources development, can be instrumental in defining and delivering organizational success. However, it is important to select those means *after* identifying what gaps in results they will close at the Micro, Macro, and Mega levels. If one selects a means before completing a proper needs assessment, the costs for doing so can be both damaging to the budget as well as to those that initiated the means.

Chapter 7
Linking Analysis and Solutions to Make Useful Recommendations

What's in This Chapter?

- A six-step model for identifying and solving problems: for getting from What Is to What Should Be

- A description of various types of analyses and their unique purposes

- Guidance for implementation, evaluation, and continuous improvement

Framework for Selecting Solutions: Six-Step Problem-Solving Model

This chapter introduces you to a series of analysis tools that help you find the best solutions for the needs you have identified as top priorities for the organization to address. One useful tool to help us conceptualize the flow of this process is Kaufman's Six-Step Problem-Solving Model (Figure 7.1).

Here's an overview of the process and the purpose behind each step:

1. We define a *problem* as a need selected for resolution. Needs assessment allows us to define the documented and evidence-based needs to be resolved. There are various analysis techniques that are also appropriate in helping you verify top priority problems, including SWOT analysis and cost-consequences analysis, described later in this chapter.

2. Causal factors are identified through a causal analysis. Later in this chapter, we will introduce various approaches to conducting a causal analysis.

3. Solution requirements stem out of the causal analysis, and allow you to identify what criteria should be met by the solution alternatives you consider.

4. You then consider a range of alternative solutions that meet the solution requirements listed in step 3, along with pros and cons. A methods-means analysis, described later in this chapter, is instrumental in this step.

5. You select the solution(s) that ranks the highest, based on a methods-means analysis, which determines what meets the criteria at the lowest costs.

6. Part of ensuring your solution is and continues to be effective is thoughtful implementation, which implies proper change management, and monitoring and evaluation that allow you to continuously improve.

The remainder of this chapter provides a detailed discussion of the various analysis tools mentioned.

Figure 7.1   Kaufman's Six-Step Problem-Solving Model

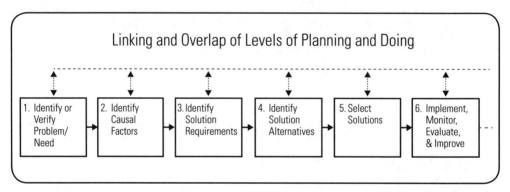

Source: Based on Kaufman, R., 2006, 2011.

Analysis Defined

Webster's Dictionary describes analysis as the process of studying the nature of something or determining its essential features and their relations. While needs assessment helps us identify the gaps in results, a *causal analysis* can help us understand why those gaps exist. It is what we learn from that causal analysis that will provide one critical dimension to consider when selecting solutions, the methods or means that will help us close those gaps.

There are, however, other analysis tools that can optimize our decision-making process throughout various stages of the needs assessment and performance improvement process. Below is an overview of the analysis tools that will be described throughout this chapter:

- *SWOT analysis:* the identification and organization of an organization's strengths, weaknesses, opportunities, and threats, with regards to a specific set of objectives. It is important to note that an organization's SWOT analysis is most useful when focused on a specific set of objectives, rather than an approach that is more general, as the SWOTs might be different for two different sets of objectives, even within one organization.

- *Cost-consequences analysis (CCA):* an analysis that looks at the costs and consequences of a given decision. The decision could be whether or not to close a gap (used in gap prioritization), or whether to select one solution alternative or another. All decisions and actions (and lack thereof) come with a set of costs and consequences. Costs can be both financial and non-financial.

- *Causal analysis:* an analysis that looks at the root causes of the gaps identified during the needs assessment. These causes will provide the basic foundation for identifying solution criteria. In order for a solution to be considered, it should meet the basic solution criteria.

- *Methods-means analysis (MMA):* provides a comparison and contrast among the various solutions that meet your solution criteria, along with additional pros and cons for each of those solutions.

SWOT Analysis

A *SWOT analysis* is a planning tool that identifies and organizes the strengths, weaknesses, opportunities, and threats of an organization. Sometimes it is even used at a project level. Here's a review of the acronym:

- *Strengths:* Internal to the organization, these are organizational attributes or characteristics that represent an important advantage.

- *Weaknesses:* Internal to the organization, these are organizational attributes or characteristics, or limitations that represent an important disadvantage for the organization.

- *Opportunities:* External to the organization, these are elements in the environment that may bring possibilities for improvement.

- *Threats:* External to the organization, these are elements in the environment that could present important challenges or difficulties for the organization.

A SWOT analysis begins with clear and valid objectives. If being carried out in the context of a Mega or strategic needs assessment and planning process, a SWOT could be used along with a CCA to help prioritize the organization's strategic or societal gaps. Therefore, it would be applied after the organization's Ideal Vision and related gaps have been identified, but prior to deriving the organizational mission objective (Kaufman, 2000).

This process can often be conducted in a facilitated discussion setting with strategic stakeholders and partners, most likely the same group you identified for your Mega-level needs assessment. Depending on the level of analysis and discussion, this may take place in a one- to two-day retreat. However, it is certainly possible to use technology (email and a range of web-based meeting and communication tools) to conduct a virtual and/or asynchronous variation of this.

Essentially, you would ask the participants to brainstorm specific ideas for each of the categories, described above. Be sure to provide clear instructions that include both the specific set of organizational objectives (or Mega-level gaps) in question as well as definitions of each of these categories. This will enhance communication and discussion efficiency by ensuring that everyone knows about what type of ideas are being sought for each category. Brainstorm as many ideas as considered important, but usually you'll be in the range of five to 10. Table 7.1 below provides a template for visually representing SWOTs, and guiding discussion.

After each of the categories are populated, you may consider relating and ranking them to get a clearer understanding of which of these will exert the most influence, and in what ways, on your target objectives. We reiterate that this is not the time for specific discussions of methods or means. Rather, this provides input to general solution requirements that will be used along with other analysis results to later identify the most effective solutions.

Table 7.1   SWOT Template

Objectives	Strengths	Weaknesses	Opportunities	Threats
1. Increase early breast cancer detection among our female clients of target age by at least 13% over the next 10 years.	• We have been offering an early breast cancer detection program for over 10 years and have a good track record for compliance (87%).	• We have not developed the right tactics to help us go beyond our 87% compliance rate for over five years.	• New legislation will make the healthcare industry more competitive. Focusing on measurable value added (and providing evidence in our marketing efforts) to our customers could be our competitive edge.	• BIC does not have complete influence over customer behavior.
2. Objective 2	etc.	etc.	etc.	etc.
3. Objective 3	etc.	etc.	etc.	etc.

Cost-Consequences Analysis (CCA)

A *cost-consequences analysis* looks at the costs and consequences of a given decision. It essentially allows us to identify chains of events that can result in undesirable consequences. The decision could be whether or not to close a gap (used in gap prioritization), or whether to select one solution or another. These costs can be both financial and non-financial.

A CCA is a powerful tool used to influence decision making. All actions, including not acting (for example, ignoring a gap) bring a set of costs and consequences. Decision makers often allow the financial costs of doing something to have overwhelming influence in their decisions.

We suggest that one way to help your needs assessment partners reconsider their decisions is to also present them, or help them identify, the costs and consequences associated with not doing that very thing, for example, of not addressing an identified gap. Identifying what can happen if no action is taken may help decision makers realize that ignoring a gap can sometimes have even higher costs.

If we establish a chain of events all the way to the Mega level of results, it often becomes clear how everything we do ultimately links to results at the Micro, Macro, and Mega level, including those specific elements of the Ideal Vision introduced in chapter 3.

A CCA may be illustrated as what is shown in Table 7.2.

Table 7.2   Example of Cost-Consequences Analysis

Gap	Costs and Consequences for Closure	Costs and Consequences for Ignoring
• 10% in professional certification	*Costs:* Financial costs of preparing/training customers and sales professionals for certification process; also, the certification exam fee. *Consequences:* Might set precedence for BIC to cover other professional certifications for other positions.	*Costs:* Financial costs in fees, loss of customers, and potential legal action. *Consequences:* Staff that are not certified could: • result in industry fines to BIC • provide erroneous information to our customers • make poor decisions about coverage. These consequences could in turn reduce customer satisfaction, customer retention, and even be detrimental to the health of our customers.

Causal Analysis

A *causal analysis* looks at the root causes of the gaps identified during the needs assessment. These causes will provide the basic foundation for identifying solution criteria. In order for a solution to be considered, it should meet the basic solution criteria.

Assessing needs before analyzing them reduces or eliminates the potential risks of assuming that what is being analyzed is the root cause of performance deficiencies.

Harless states "If, in fact, Performance Technology is 'goal-driven,' then it makes sense that an early step in the methodology ('process') of Performance Technology is to address the question: *What is the basic business/personal/societal goal relevant to the current situation?"* (1992, p. 5). A similar approach to this adapted model was described by Rummler (1999). Rummler lists and describes a performance improvement approach based on the traditional ADDIE model; however, before analysis can be carried out, he proposes that as a first step, the problem or opportunity must be defined. Although the specific needs assessment tasks proposed by Kaufman are not all incorporated into Rummler's first step, he does make the distinction between the problem definition phase and the analysis phase.

Similarly, Stolovitch, Keeps, and Rodrigue (1999) also make the distinction between an assessment phase and the analysis phase by listing the performance improvement phases as: problem or opportunity definition, conducting analysis, designing and developing the intervention, implementing and maintaining the intervention, and evaluating the intervention.

This distinction allows practitioners the opportunity to identify root problems and the appropriate interventions, with a lower probability of bias toward a comfortable method. It is critical to validly justify and demonstrate that the recommended solutions are appropriate for achieving the client's objectives (see Dean, 1999; Clark and Estes, 2000; Kaufman and Clark, 1999; Stolovtich, 2000; Westgaard, 1988).

There are a variety of performance improvement models that include both assessment and analysis components, primarily at the Micro level (for example, Harless, 1970; Mager and Pipe, 1970; Robinson and Robinson, 1995; and Rothwell, 1996). Another respected model is that offered by Rummler (1995), which actually links Macro, Micro, and Process levels with an assessment and analysis process. Ultimately, all of these models consistently identify the same general category of causal factors affecting human performance in organization around issues relating to 1) expectations and standards, 2) work support and tools, 3) motivation and feedback, and 4) selection and ability.

Based on this logic, all things being equal, chances are that instructional solutions would be appropriate for roughly 20 percent of performance problems (Trinner, Greenberry, and Watkins, 1996).

Perhaps the most quintessential and most widely used analysis models at the performer level are Mager and Pipe's (1970) Performance Analysis Model and Gilbert's (1978) Behavioral Engineering Model. For this reason, an overview and relevant guides are provided below as job aids for your analysis.

Gilbert proposed the Behavior Engineering Model, based on what he termed the Third Leisurely Theorem, or Management Theorem, which states:

For any given accomplishment, a deficiency in performance always has as its immediate cause a deficiency in a behavior repertory, or in the environment that supports the repertory, or in both. But its ultimate cause will be found in a deficiency of the management system (p.76).

This two-dimensional (individual and environment) model addresses six elements, categorized under three main groups, which may affect performance. These elements are data, instruments, incentives, knowledge, response capacity, and motives (see Table 7.3). For organizational settings, Gilbert suggested that addressing the first three factors would most likely lead to improved performance, as "the environment is easier to manipulate than people's repertoires" (p.86). In essence, Gilbert considers this model as "an outline of a performance troubleshooting sequence," which should begin with cell 1 of Table 7.3 and proceed to address the elements of the remaining cells in a sequential order. This model has served as the foundation for many performance improvement strategies and tools.

Mager and Pipe's Performance Analysis is represented as a flowchart that guides the entire performance improvement process by asking a series of questions beginning with a description of the performance discrepancy and ending in the selection of an appropriate intervention.

Following the conventional emphasis on analysis, the authors offer the model as a procedure that "shows how to analyze the nature, the importance and the cause of things called performance discrepancies" (1970, p.5). A discrepancy can occur between someone's actual performance and the desired performance (analogous to a Micro-level needs assessment). Subsequently, one of the first steps in the process is to identify the nature of the discrepancy, and then consider its importance (analogous to the process of gap prioritization we presented in chapters 3, 4, 5, and 6). If the discrepancy is not important, they suggest it should be ignored. If it is important, one should determine if it is due to a genuine skill deficiency, since this is so often the most common requests by clients. A series of questions are posed until one can consider solutions and compare the size of the remedy with the size of the discrepancy.

Table 7.3   The Behavioral Engineering Model

	S^D Information	R Instrumentation	Sr Motivation
E **Environmental** **Supports**	Data • Are roles and performance expectations clearly defined? • Are employees given relevant and frequent feedback about the adequacy of their performance? • Do they have descriptions of what performance is expected? • Are there clear and relevant guides to adequate performance?	Instruments • Do they have materials, tools, and time to do the job? • Process and procedures are clearly defined and enhance performance, if followed? • Is the work environment safe and supportive? For example, organized, safe, clean, etc.?	Incentives • Are there adequate financial incentives made contingent upon performance? • Are nonmonetary incentives made available based on performance? For example, career development opportunities? Recognition and encouragement? Are jobs enriched to fulfill the needs of employees themselves?
P **Person's repertory** **of behavior**	Knowledge • Do they have the right sets of skills and knowledge to do the job? Do they have proper training to do the job? • Are employees placed in the right job? • Are employees cross-trained to understand each other's jobs?	Capacity • Do employees have the innate physical, mental, and emotional capabilities to do the job? • Were they properly selected for the job, based on their demonstrated past accomplishments?	Motives • Do you understand what motivates people to work or not work? • Do you know if they have the internal desire to do the job? • Were they properly selected for the job, based on their own personal goals?

Source: Based on Gilbert, 1978.

Figure 7.1 is a flowchart depicting this process. Key questions that guide a Mager and Pipe approach to causal analysis, based on their 1997 checklist, appear in Table 7.4.

In spite of being one of the most widely used models, it has received two strong criticisms. First, the flowchart representation suggests to some that the process is linear, and secondly, it fails to place performance in a larger context (Wedman and Graham, 1998). Both of these limitations can of course be countered by linking them to a formal needs assessment at the Mega, Macro, or Micro level, as described previously in this book. The results of your analysis is then presented to your needs assessment and planning partners (preferably in in the context of a meeting where you can explain your findings and respond to their questions), providing also a series of performance requirements that would be used as the criteria to be used in your MMA (described later in this chapter).

Table 7.4   Mager and Pipe Questions for Performance Analysis Process

Key Questions	Exploratory Questions
A. They are not doing what they should be doing. I think I've got a training problem.	
1. What is the performance discrepancy? (Describe actual and desired performance similar to a micro-level needs assessment. Are the expectations for performance clear?)	• Why do I think there is a training problem? • What is the difference between what is being done and what is supposed to be done? • What is the event that causes me to say that things aren't right? • Why am I dissatisfied?
2. Is it important? (Is it worth pursuing? What evidence suggest that it is? If not, drop it.)	• Why is the discrepancy important? • What would happen if I left the discrepancy alone? • Would doing something to resolve the discrepancy have any worthwhile result?
3. Is it a skill deficiency?	• Could the person do it if it really required to do it? • Could the person do it if his or her life depended on it? • Are the person's present skills adequate for the desired performance?
B. Yes. It is a skill deficiency. They couldn't do it if their lives depended on it.	
4. Could they do it in the past?	• Did the person once know how to perform as desired? • Has the person forgotten how to do what I want done?
5. Is the skill used often? (Are performance consequences and feedback used effectively?)	• How often is the skill or performance used? • Is there regular feedback on performance? • Exactly how does the person find out how well he or she is doing?
6. Is there a simpler solution? (Can the task be made easier?)	• Can I change the job by providing some kind of job aid? • Can I store the required information some way (in written instructions, checklists) other than in someone's head? • Can I show (demonstrate) rather than train? • Would informal (such as on-the-job) training be sufficient?
7. Do they have what it takes? (Does the person have the potential to do the task?)	• Could the person learn the job (is the individual trainable)? • Does this person have the physical and mental potential to perform as desired? • Is this person overqualified for the job?

Continued on next page.

Table 7.4 continued.

C. Is it not a skill deficiency. They could do it if they wanted to.	
8. Is the desired performance punishing?	• What is the consequence of performing as desired? • Is it punishing to perform as expected?	• Does the person perceive desired performance as being geared toward penalties? • Would the person's world become a little dimmer if the desired performance were attained?
9. Is non-performance rewarding?	• What is the result of doing it the present way instead of my way? • What does the person get out of the present performance in the way of reward, prestige, status, jollies? • Does the person get more attention for misbehaving than behaving?	• What event in the world supports (i.e. rewards) the present way of doing things? (Am I inadvertently rewarding irrelevant behavior while overlooking the crucial behaviors?) • Is this person "mentally inadequate," doing less so that there is less to worry about? • Is this person physically inadequate, e.g., doing less because it is less tiring?
10. Does performing really matter to them?	• Does performing as desired matter to the performer? • Is there a favorable outcome for performing? • Is there an undesirable outcome for not performing?	• Is there a source of satisfaction for performing? • Can this person take pride in this performance as an individual or as a member of a group? • Is there a personal satisfaction from the job?
11. Are there obstacles to performing? (Are the resources adequate?)	• What prevents this person from performing? • Does the person know what is expected? • Does the person know how to do what is expected? • Does the person know when to do what is expected? • Are there conflicting demands on this person's time? • Does the person lack the authority, time, or tools?	• Are there restrictive policies, or a "right way of doing it," or a "way we've always done it" that ought to be changed? • Can I reduce interference by improving lighting, changing colors, increasing comfort, modifying the work position, or reducing visual or auditory distractions? • Can I reduce "competition from the job," such as phone calls, "brush fires," demands of less important but more immediate problems?
D. What should I do now?	
12. Which solution is best?	• Have all the potential solutions been identified? • Does each solution address itself to one or more problems identified during the analysis (such as skill deficiency, absence of potential, incorrect rewards, punishing consequences, distracting obstacles)? • What is the cost of each potential solution? • Have the intangible costs been assessed? • Which solution is most practical, feasible, and economical?	• Which solution will add most value (solve the largest part of the problem with the least effort)? • Which remedy is likely to give us the most results for the least effort? • Which solutions are we best equipped to try? • Which remedy interests us most? (Or, which remedy is most visible to those who must be satisfied?)

Source: Based on Mager and Pipe, 1997 (permission to print granted by R. Mager).

Consider, for example, if our analysis findings of BIC sales and service professionals' performance gap revealed the following causes, depicted in Table 7.5.

Table 7.5   Link Between Gap, Causal Factor, and Performance Results

Performance Gap	Causal Factors	Performance Requirement/Intention
• There is a gap of 10 new accounts acquired per month (desired 20, current 10).	• Roles and performance specifications are not clearly defined. • Sales and service professionals are not given relevant and frequent feedback about the adequacy of their performance. • Some job aids are obsolete, inconsistent, or irrelevant to the job.	• Must increase sales and service acquisition of at least 10 new accounts per month. • Sales and service professionals must receive relevant, frequent, and corrective feedback about the adequacy of their performance. • Job aids must be current and directly related to meeting specific performance objectives. All job aids will be consistent with one another.

Look at it this way: You wouldn't hire the first person that walked off the street, just because they popped into your office. You would first determine what the functions, experiences, and educational requirements a new employee would have to fulfill to contribute to the objectives of the team, department, organization, and so on. Likewise, the job candidate (solution) that is recommended has to meet certain "job qualifications," and if he meets them all, or at least the most important ones (sometimes this is the most practical way to go and still get the job done), only then does he get employed (or the solution implemented).

Methods-Means Analysis and Solution Selection

Methods-means analysis (MMA) provides a comparison and contrast among the various solutions that meet your solution criteria, along with additional pros and cons for each of those solutions (Kaufman, 2000).

A methods-means analysis is best conducted in a work session with your needs assessment and planning partners, and could immediately follow your presentation of the causal analysis findings and solution criteria.

The process is straightforward:

1. **List the solution requirements** for a given need. This should have been identified as the last part of your causal analysis.

2. **List potential solutions** that meet the criteria. Brainstorm a variety of alternatives, using the solution specifications as the parameters for the ideas.

3. **List pros and cons** for each potential solution. For each identified alternative, consider the pros and cons. Do the pros outweigh the cons? This question is not only about the number of pros versus cons, but also about their importance. There may be only one apparent pro weighed against five cons, but if that one pro is, for instance, "it directly supports saving lives," it will likely outweigh the cons and costs. In the next step, ranking them, you can compare the alternatives to determine whether you can get the same level of pros in an alternative, for perhaps lower costs (again, financial and non-financial).

4. **Rank order** the solutions in terms of their ability to meet most criteria and have their pros outweigh their cons. With this information at hand, we are in the position to rank the alternatives in order of appropriateness and feasibility. What is appropriate and feasible will vary from organization to organization. Your partners may also want a list of pertinent criteria that makes sense for their own organization and purposes.

5. **Select the solution** (from among alternatives). After ranking, the needs assessment partners will ultimately have to decide which alternatives make the most sense, and take accountability for the costs and consequences of those selected solutions. Your primary role is to facilitate the process, and while you can certainly provide your view, the needs assessor does not pick the solutions or make ultimate decisions. This is part of establishing accountability for decision makers.

Table 7.6 depicts a methods-means analysis summary template for BIC.

Implementation, Monitoring, Evaluation, and Improvement

Implementation

The success of a given solution in solving a performance problem, or meeting a need, is not guaranteed by merely selecting the right solution set, though that is a prerequisite. Also important to the success of a selected solution is how well it is implemented. That is, how well the change is managed. This is an often neglected step, and one key reason for why the "right" solution can fail. Two things that will help you ensure the success of your solutions are:

Table 7.6 Methods-Means Analysis (MMA) Template

Gap/Need: *There is a gap of 10 new accounts acquired per month (desired 20, current 10).*			
Solution Requirements	**Solution Alternatives**	**Pros**	**Cons**
• Must increase sales and service acquisition of at least 10 new accounts per month. • Sales and service professionals must receive clear, accomplishment-driven expectations. • Sales and service professionals must receive relevant, frequent, and corrective feedback about the adequacy of their performance. • Job aids must be current and directly related to meeting specific performance objectives. All job aids will be consistent with one another.	*Alternative 1:* Revamp entire performance management system for sales and service professionals that align expectations, on-the-job support, evaluation, and feedback.	• One comprehensive solution that could be specifically designed and deployed to focus on new account acquisition. • The same performance management system could be designed with multiple sales and service accomplishments in mind (leveraging it for multiple purposes). • High long-term return-on-investment. • Should also improve sales and service professionals' morale and job satisfaction. • Meets most solution requirements.	• Currently, we don't have anything integrated in place because we don't have the expertise. We would have to pay consultant fees to help us design such a system. • Will also require training for all of those responsible for 'managing' performance with the system. • High up-front financial cost.
	Alternative 2: Outsource customer service roles, and keep 'sales representatives.'	• We will have sales reps focused solely on sales. • Will help control costs.	• Customer relationships could be compromised since sales professionals will not be accountable for overall customer satisfaction with BIC. • Having non-employees deal with our customers takes some quality control away from us. Could negatively impact BIC's image.
	Alternative 3: Outsource aggressive sales training from a sales training vendor.	• Have current relationship with external vendor who offers top sales professionals as trainers.	• Not sure if and how training will transfer well to the job. • Already engaged in training updates for new legislation compliance. This might fragment our overall development program as opposed to making it seamless.

- create and implement a communication plan
- create and implement a robust change management plan.

Create and implement a communication plan. Determine target populations that will be affected in any way by the changes in the process. Determine how best to communicate with each and what each has to know when. Create communication methods and vehicles. Deploy communication methods and vehicles and measure the effectiveness of all communications and adjust as required.

Create and implement a robust change management plan. Determine what jobs or tasks will be changing. Determine how other performance improvement interventions may be affected. Identity specific employees who will be directly and indirectly affected by the changes. Determine if training, coaching, job aids, or other performance support tools will be required to support the effectiveness of the new solution. Ensure that performance management system reflects required changes. Ensure managers and other workforce leaders understand how to support performance with the new solution(s).

Monitoring, Evaluation, and Continual Improvement

The point of conducting a needs assessment is to measurably improve what the organization delivers to external clients. However, improvement is not a one-time deal. The world is continuously changing, and in order for us to remain proactive, we must not only respond to change, but also anticipate and even create it.

Continual improvement demands that we know where we are headed (our direction is set by a needs assessment), and continually monitor our course from where we are to where we want to be. We do this by asking the right questions, collecting useful data on an ongoing basis, and then applying that data to make sound decisions about required changes or which current initiatives to sustain. There are two major components to continual improvement: monitoring and adjusting. *Monitoring* is about measuring and tracking data relevant to the objectives we want reach, and what influence the solutions we implemented are exerting over those objectives. We measure what matters and track its progress. This is essentially what formative evaluation is about. It helps us improve as we travel toward a desired destination, so that we can have a more efficient trip. Performance dashboards offer an excellent way to monitor and track our objectives. Chapter 9 will discuss they key elements of useful performance dashboards.

Adjusting is about change. We use the feedback obtained from the monitoring stage to create, promote, and facilitate desirable change. With a clear idea of the change we want to create in our organizations, we can then ensure a most effective and efficient change process by following the same guidelines provided in the previous section.

Summative evaluation, then, allows you to confirm whether or not you reached the desired destination. It is essentially the other side of the coin from needs assessment. While needs assessment identifies gaps between where we are and where we want to be, summative evaluation determines gaps between where we are and where we said we wanted to be. Chapter 8 provides a more in-depth discussion on the linkages between needs assessment and evaluation.

Chapter Summary

This chapter introduced the Six-Step Problem-Solving Model as a framework that ties the various performance improvement steps. In this context, various types of analysis and models were also presented, as compliments to the preliminary needs assessment phase. We also introduced guidelines for implementation, evaluation, and continual improvement which will be further discussed in the next chapter.

Chapter 8
Linking Needs Assessment to Evaluation

What's in This Chapter?

- A clear definition of evaluation

- The relationship between needs assessment and evaluation

- The purpose of formative and summative evaluation

- How the Impact Evaluation Process and OEM are directly linked

As mentioned in the previous chapter, both needs assessment and evaluation are integral parts of continual improvement. Needs assessment helps us set direction; evaluation, in its formative sense, helps us track our direction, and in the summative sense, helps us confirm whether or not we have arrived and met our objectives while reducing or eliminating our priority needs.

Evaluation: Definition and Purpose

The fundamental purpose of evaluation, from our perspective, is to help us make data-driven decisions that lead to improved performance of programs and organizations. Each and every component of the evaluation must be aligned with those objectives and expectations that the organization values, and the decisions that will have to be made as a result of the evaluation findings. These decisions are essentially concerned with how to measurably improve performance at all levels of the organization: internal deliverables, organizational gains, and societal impact. At its core, evaluation is simple:

- It compares results with expectations or intentions.

- It finds drivers and barriers to expected performance.

- It produces action plans for improving the programs and solutions being evaluated so that expected performance is achieved or maintained, so that organizational objectives and contributions can be realized (Guerra-Lopez, 2008).

As noted in the previous chapter, there are two main types of evaluations, based on Scriven (1967): formative and summative. Formative evaluation typically occurs during the developmental stage of a program and can be used to improve the program before it is formally launched and during development and implementation. Of course, the formative approach can be used to improve all stages of performance improvement from assessment to implementation, and to the evaluation itself.

Summative Evaluation

Summative evaluation occurs after the implementation of a program or solution and usually requires some amount of time to have transpired so that the object of evaluation has the opportunity to have the full impact required on performance at various levels of the organization. It is worth noting that summative evaluation can also be used to improve programs and solutions. Stufflebeam and Webster (1980) hold that the objectives-based view of program evaluation is the most common type of evaluation.

Just like with needs assessment, once the results accomplished have been determined, the evaluator is well advised to also identify causal factors contributing to such results. These data should provide insights as to what the drivers and barriers to the success of the program are, thereby providing the basis for recommendations for improving performance. Needs assessments are proactive—they define and justify the future to be delivered. Evaluation is reactive in that it determines what has been accomplished based on the actions taken and on the needs identified and selected.

While there are approaches to evaluation that do not focus on predetermined results or objectives, the approach we propose is based on the premise of performance improvement. The underlying assumption is that organizations, whether fully articulated or not, expect specific results and contributions from programs and other solutions; they have to prove that what they do and deliver is worth the price. This does not prevent the evaluator or performance improvement professional from employing means to help them identify unanticipated results and consequences. The worth or merit of programs and solutions is then determined by whether or not they delivered desired results, whether these results are worth having in the first place, and whether the benefits of these results outweigh their costs and unintended consequences. Evaluation should be used for fixing and improving and never for blaming.

An evaluation, one that asks and answers the right questions, can be used not only to determine results, but also to explain why results were found to be such and how to modify that which is being evaluated, so that it can meet the intended objectives within the required criteria. This is useful not only to identify what went wrong or what could be better, but also to identify what should be maintained. Through Appreciative Inquiry, evaluation can help us identify what is going right. *Appreciative Inquiry* is a process that searches for the best in organizations to find opportunities for performance improvement and creation (Cooperrider and Srivastva, 1987). Here too the efforts are but a means to an end, improving performance.

Formative Evaluation

Formative evaluation can be designed in such a way that it continuously monitors the alignment of a program with its subsystems and suprasystems to facilitate the achievement of its ultimate value.

Formative evaluation should start along with the identification, design, development, and implementation of the program or solution of interest, and it can even start alongside the needs assessment. Some general questions that would guide a formative evaluation include (Guerra-López, 2007):

- Are we targeting the right objectives?
    - Are they based on assessed needs (gaps in results)?
- Are the criteria measurable and soundly based?
    - Are we using the right criteria to judge the effectiveness and efficiency of our solution?
- Did we identify the appropriate program or solution?
    - Did we base our selection on an analysis of alternatives?
    - Did we weigh the pros and cons?
    - Did we weigh the costs and consequences?
- Is our design useful and relevant?
    - Is the design aligned with the front-end analysis findings (causes for gaps in results)?
    - Is our design appropriate for the ends we want to reach?

- Is the development of the program/solution aligned with its intended design?

  - Is our pilot designed to capture the right data required for improvements?

  - Does our prototype meet the requirements of our users?

  - Based on our progress, are there things we use and do that should be revised and changed now in order for us to deliver the results we promised?

- Is the program/solution being implemented appropriately?[1]

  - Were those affected by the program/solution included in the problem identification, solution selection, and every other stage?

  - Were fears and unfounded ideas about the implications of the program/solution confronted, clarified, and/or disproved, as appropriate?

  - Is the program/solution being implemented according to initial plans?

  - If the implementation of the program/solution responsive and flexible to the current situation (including challenges not previously foreseen)?

Evaluating each stage, and using evaluation data to improve them, will allow evaluators and stakeholders to stay on track to reach the short- and long-term objectives of the program or solution.

Linking Needs Assessment and Evaluation

The Impact Evaluation Process

As we discussed in chapter 2, Kaufman's Organizational Elements Model provided the differentiation between the three basic levels of results, as well as the important distinction between means and end. With this as the overarching conceptual framework, in the Impact Evaluation Process, the solutions we evaluate are always considered means to an end, with the end manifesting itself in three levels of results: *Mega, Macro,* and *Micro.* This is essentially the idea that any solution must ultimately have a positive impact on the Mega level, but in the short- and mid-term, you must begin to align and measure the solutions' influence over the Micro and Macro levels.

---

1. Incidentally, implementation questions may also be appropriate during the summative evaluation approach, where we don't only look at the results and consequences, but we also look at the factors that may have impacted those results and consequences (e.g. implementation issues). Obviously, if our intent is to ensure the effectiveness of the solution, we want to know if we are implementing it effectively before and during implementation, not just after the fact.

Scriven's consumer-oriented evaluation approach is consistent with this view, in that Scriven (1991) argues that rather than accepting a developer's goals as given, the evaluation must judge whether the achievement of the goals would contribute to the welfare of clients and consumers. Regardless of the products and outputs, Scriven argues that the evaluators must also identity outcomes and determine their value as they relate to the consumer's needs.[2]

If a needs assessment was conducted, and it was done well, then there should be a high probability that the solution selected on the basis of hard data will in fact add positive and measurable value to the organization and its customers through its various levels of results. In other words, the solution should have been selected in light of needs (gaps in results) prioritized (based on the cost and consequences associated with meeting the needs versus ignoring them) at the Micro, Macro, and Mega levels, and the pros and cons associated with each alternative considered for closing such gaps (recall that the solution alternatives come directly from a need/ causal analysis, the process by which root causes of the identified needs are found). If the selected solution was the best alternative for closing the gap, then one summative evaluation hypothesis is that the solution should have helped eliminate or reduce such gaps in results or performance. The basic evaluation question, from a summative perspective, would then be: *Did solution* x *contribute to the reduction or elimination of performance gap* y?

Consistently, Scriven also calls for identifying and ranking the alternative programs or solutions that are available based on the relative costs and effects, and in consideration of the needs identified through a needs assessment based on societal value added. Additionally, the Impact Evaluation Process is also influenced by decision-oriented theory, and Patton's (1997) utilization-focused evaluation, an approach to evaluation concerned with designing evaluations that inform decision making.

The Impact Evaluation Process consists of seven elements, that while convey sequence, can be considered reiteratively. The basic steps and approach are illustrated in Figure 8.1, and each of its seven phases is described in more detail below.

1. Identify Stakeholders and Expectations. The process begins with the evaluator's identification of the key stakeholders involved. Perhaps it may be composed of many of the same individuals that were part of your needs assessment team. Recall that the stakeholder group includes those who will be making decisions either throughout the evaluation process, or directly as a result of the evaluation findings.

---

2. It is important to note that Scriven never differentiated needs from wants, as we do in this book.

Figure 8.1 The Impact Evaluation Process

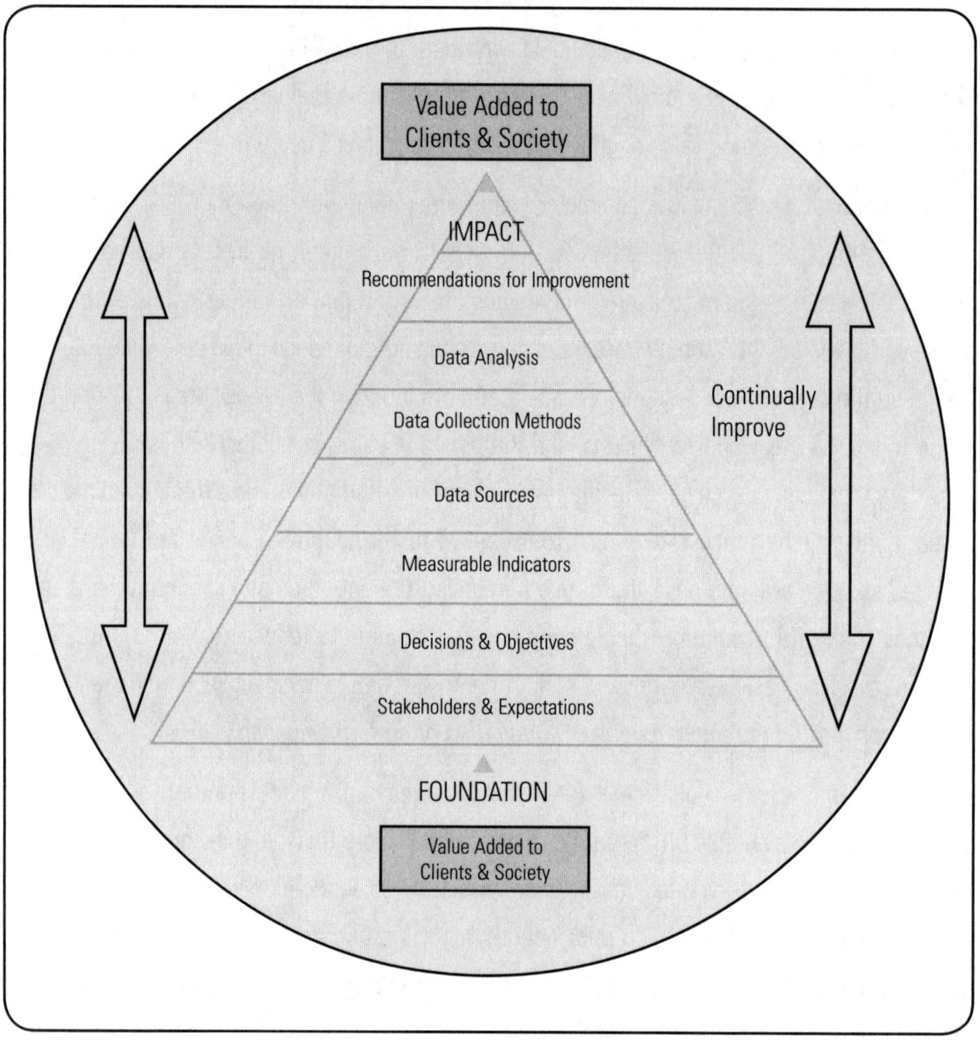

Source: Guerra-López, I, 2007.

Those with the authority to make critical decisions are often the ones who finance the evaluation project, but if it is someone else or some other group, they too should be included. Also important are those who will be affected by the evaluation—either in the process, or potentially as a result of the findings. Including this group will make the implementation of the evaluation plan a lot easier, particularly during the data collection stage. You may think of other stakeholders who are important to your particular situation. The driving question for identifying stakeholders is: *Who is (or could be) either affected by the evaluation, or could potentially affect the evaluation in a meaningful way?*

It should be noted that each stakeholder group may have its own set of expectations. While some of these expectations might overlap, some will be particular to the vantage point and respective interests of a given group. Relevant expectation areas include specific evaluation questions to be answered, timeframes, final report content and format-related issues, and data and observation access, among others. One common element that should tie in these individual expectations is the organizational vision, which should be based on external impact on society. Otherwise, each stakeholder group might end up pulling in separate directions, leaving the organization no better (or worse) than it was before.

This process purports that if the evaluator does not clearly identify the expectations and requirements of stakeholders, it is nearly impossible to meet those expectations and requirements. Even if a good evaluation, technically speaking, was conducted, it will not add any value if it was misaligned to stakeholder expectations and adding value to all internal and external stakeholders. Evaluation data and results that are not relevant, and thus not used, waste everyone's time and resources.

Thus, it is critical that one understands how a successful evaluation—and evaluator—will be judged by stakeholders. Here are some general questions that should be answered before proceeding:

- What decisions do they wish to make as a result of your final deliverable(s)?
- What is expected of the evaluator?
- What is expected of the evaluation project?
- How will your performance as an evaluator be judged?
- What will the communication process be? With whom? How often?
  Through what medium?
- What will be expected of stakeholders (specifically, what type of support will they provide to you: feedback, data collection assistance, administrative, other)?
- What will be the impact of applying the evaluation results or not applying them?

Also critical is that you align stakeholder expectations with external societal demands. While not all stakeholders might see the links as easily, it is your responsibility to clarify those linkages. It is not a matter of whether or not such linkages exist for this particular organization; instead, it is how well you can, together, clarify and communicate those linkages and consequences. This is the only way all of you can see clearly where you are headed, and how the programs or solutions you are evaluating affect that journey: where you were headed and how to tell if you arrived.

These expectations then become the basis for the contract, whether verbal or written, and should explicitly articulate what is expected of both the evaluator and stakeholders. If anyone feels the expectations are unreasonable, this is the time to discuss and come to a consensus; certainly not after the evaluator has completed what in her own mind is a successful evaluation.

2. Determine Key Decisions and Objectives. Along with the identification of stakeholders, another important early step is to identify the decisions that will have to be made with the evaluation findings. Asking the stakeholders to think carefully about these decisions early in the process will help the evaluator focus on the important issues, and lead them to useful data (Watkins and Guerra, 2003).

For instance, a decision might be whether to roll out a new incentive program to other branches of a bank, after its implementation in one of the branches. This decision would be based on a number of criteria, one of which might be whether the performance goals were reached. Another criterion might be whether the goals were accomplished within the required timeframe. Yet another might be whether the benefits of the new incentive program outweighed the costs. Was there an unintended effect on other parts of the performance system? As you can see, these issues are pertinent to determining the (net) worth of the intervention.

The discussion about the decisions that must be made is should be also be about the objectives that must be reached. All organizations have objectives—both external and internal—and everything within the organization must contribute toward those objectives (Guerra, 2005). The relative worth of any program or solution is primarily contingent on whether it is helping or hindering the achievement of organizational performance objectives and external contributions.

While some stakeholders may not provide the evaluator with the specific results they expect, they will provide clues about the relevant effects they are expecting, even if these are about means rather than results. The evaluator's task here, and throughout the entire process, is to be the *educator* and *facilitator*, and approach the conversation from the standpoint of...*and if we were to accomplish that, what would the result be?* This line of inquiry should continue until key results have been identified.

Of course one key source of the expected results of an intervention is the actual gaps and objectives that were documented through a needs assessment process, and which were supposed to have been addressed through this solution. Take a look at a past needs assessment report, if there is one. This document should include the initial problem, why this solution was recommended, and what specific objectives it is supposed to meet. With these decisions and objectives clarified, the overarching questions that will drive the evaluation process, and purpose of the evaluation, should also become clear, articulated, and agreed upon. Figure 8.1 reflects nested relationships among the seven phases of the Impact Evaluation Process, with stakeholders and external impact on society as the basis for everything done in an evaluation. The evaluator will not always start out with a clear purpose. Sometimes, the decisions that have to be made are more prominent (for example, to continue to fund a program or not), and sometimes, they start out with specific questions (What impact is this program having on employee retention? What is the return-on-investment of this program?). Whatever the form your initial information is in, the evaluation will be more effective if the important details are clarified before proceeding.

Sound decisions should be primarily driven by relevant (related to results of interest), reliable (trustworthy), and valid (a true measure of what you want to measure) data, and these data should come from measurable indicators of the results we want to accomplish, which in turn are related to the questions we want to answer. Very similar to what we did during the needs assessment phase.

For useful evaluation to take place, specific expectations of the evaluation partners should be aligned with the Ideal Vision and a related mission. In a formal needs assessment or evaluation process, this would be used as the basis for deriving relevant measurable indicators of quality of life and other Ideal Vision elements. It is particularly important that all those involved in actually planning, executing, and evaluating at all levels of the organization understand this; however, the language used to articulate this Ideal Vision may not always include the details.

Remember, Ideal Vision is about the ideal ultimate destination for our shared society, not about what we commit to deliver by the end of next year. As such, its primary purpose is to guide the organization and all its members towards a common, long-term, strategic destination. Thus, the first general question we want to ask from an evaluation perspective is: *How much closer to the Ideal Vision and our mission did we get as a result of the solution(s) we implemented?* From this general question would stem other vision- or strategy-driven evaluation questions. For example, *How well are we meeting the needs (not just wants) of our clients?*

Another general evaluation question to ask at this level is: *What mission results did our solution(s) help us accomplish?* Other specific evaluation questions stem from this level; for example: *Did the solution we implemented have an impact on our profits?* Lastly, there are a number of internal building block results that, when properly linked, deliver the mission. These internal results are sometimes delivered by individual units, cross-sectional special teams, or perhaps individuals.

For example, if the solution we implemented was intended to increase job satisfaction of sales and service professionals at the Bewell Insurance Company (BIC), our evaluation question might simply be: *Did solution* x *result in an increase in sales and service professionals' job satisfaction?* Relevant indicators might include:

- decreased undesired turn-over rate by at least 30 percent

- decreased absenteeism rate by at least 10 percent

- increased scores of employee satisfaction surveys from a 3.0 average to at least a 4.5

- decrease/elimination of discrimination lawsuits filed by employees against BIC to zero.

Remember, the specific figures targeted should be derived from a needs assessment process, and the means used to achieve them will in great part depend on the causal factors that contribute to these indicators being at less than desirable levels. The general question at this level would be: *Did we accomplish that which we set out to accomplish?*

It is essential that we tie stakeholder questions to important results at the various levels. There will undoubtedly be questions about means (better, faster, bigger-type questions), and these should not be dismissed, but rather linked to those results through useful questions. This could be viewed as an opportunity for the evaluator to educate stakeholders about how to create value chains. The guiding question, in this case is: *If it is faster, what measurable benefit has it added for the organization, external stakeholders (including society), and our internal stakeholders as well?*

This type of discussion should help the stakeholders come to their own conclusions about what is truly important. It is imperative that we help them focus on the results and consequences of the solution, as that is what speaks to its effectiveness. The means associated with it speak about its efficiency, and that is not enough.

3. Deriving Measurable and Valid Indicators. Sound decisions are made on the basis of relevant, reliable, and valid data related to desired results, and the related questions we want to answer (Guerra, 2003). Therefore, the heart of an evaluation will be gathering the data required to answer the questions that guide the inquiry. People often end up making judgments based on wrong or incomplete data, particularly when they try to force connections between inappropriate data and the decisions that must be made. This is the mistake we make when we automatically rely on existing data for answers simply because the data are already there, rather than because we have carefully considered whether they are relevant, reliable, valid, and timely.

Indicators are essentially observable phenomena that are linked to something that is not directly observed and can provide information that will answer an evaluation question. They could also be the measurable criteria that you identified in your objectives (see chapter 2). Results are not always neatly and directly observed, and indicators can help us measure those results. We collect data on those indicators, in order to answer evaluation questions about whether or not some desired result was reached.

Data could include account retention rates, production rates, incident reports, content mastered and applied from training or other Human Resource Development (HRD) efforts, questionnaire results, observation notes, opinion polls, profit and loss statistics, deaths, injuries, bankruptcies, successful lawsuits, awards, and the like. These all meet the definition of data (these all could take place in the flow of events under study or they are relevant to the study by some chain of logic or rationale). However, all data may not carry the same weight in reaching conclusions and some data may be misleading due to bias of one kind or another. Here are some criteria to consider (based on Guerra-López, 2008; Guerra-López and Norris-Thomas, 2011):

- **Relevant:** directly related to the questions (overarching and specific) we must answer.

- **Reliable:** rigorously measured, trustworthy, and consistent over time.

- **Valid:** true indicators of the results we want to measure; measures what we should be measuring.

- **Complete:** Does the data set accurately represent the independently verifiable reality that you will use to make decisions?

4. Identifying Data Sources. With a list of specific indicators for which to collect data, the evaluator must first determine where she can find those data. People can likely find the data that they are looking for right in their own organizations. Existing records about past and current performance may already be available, but collected by different parties in the organization and for different reasons. The best place to start is here, as it could make the process a lot more efficient. Examples include strategic plans, business plans, consulting studies, performance reports, financial analysis reports, newsletters, and even past evaluation records.

The Internet and advances in telecommunications and other technologies allow us to link to reports, documents, databases, experts, and other sources not previously possible. For example, social indicators such as those related to quality of life (average income levels, divorce rates, crime levels, and the like) can often be found in Chambers of Commerce archives, census reports, police records, and community quality of life reports, many of which are available electronically. Others, such as those related to the environment (pollution, corporate toxic waste, to name a couple), could also be obtained from the Environmental Protection Agency (EPA), as well as from studies published in scientific journals. A number of other government agencies and research institutions, nationally and internationally, also publish a series of official studies and reports that could prove to be valuable sources of data.

Other sources may include experts, employees, and leadership. There are a number of other potential data sources you can use, but the source the evaluator selects will be dependent on the type of data she is looking for.

5. Selecting Data Collection Instruments. The right data collection methods and tools are a function of the data required. Likewise, the quality of the data one collects is a function of the methods selected. When evaluators limit the data they collect by employing a narrow set of observation methods based on the way it has always been done or personal preference, problems arise (see Kaufman, Guerra, and Platt, 2006).

The fundamental consideration in selecting appropriate data collection tools is the required data itself. If you are after hard data such as sales figures, don't use a survey to get people's opinions of what these sales figures are. Rather, review relevant sales reports. Conversely, if it is people's attitudes that are required, there are a number of ways to ask them (interviews, focus groups, and surveys are some appropriate possibilities). There is extensive literature about these and other data collection methods. The evaluator should make the selection based on their pros and cons, specifically with regards to important criteria such as appropriateness of the instrument for the required data, time, characteristics of sample, comprehensiveness of tool, previous experience with tools that are being considered, and feasibility, among others. The "secret ingredient" for successfully collecting valid and reliable data is *alignment* of data type, data source, data collection tool, and later data analysis procedures.

6. Selecting Data Analysis Tools. There are a number of quantitative analysis techniques available, but selecting the appropriate technique depends not only on the scale used to measure the data, but also on the specific purpose of your analysis. Is your intent to show the relative position of an individual in a group (measures of central tendency), for example: *Which salesperson stands apart from the rest of the team?* Or is it to describe the shape of a data set (measures of variability), for example: *Are the sales figures pretty consistent for this branch, or do individual salespeople's figures vary significantly from one another?* Or is it to show relative ranking (measures of central tendency), for example: *How do Jane Doe's performance scores stack up against her group?*

There is more to evaluation than the data collection. Considerable planning should take place prior to the actual data collection, as well as analysis, synthesis, and interpretation of the data afterward. The *analysis* of data in the evaluation effort is the organization of data to discover patterns used to support hypotheses, conclusions, or evaluative claims that result from the evaluation study in order to provide useful information to make good decisions.

One basic purpose of using statistics in evaluations is that they enable large amounts of data to be sensibly and clearly summarized. Under this category there are two basic measures. One is the measure of central tendency, which includes the mean, median, and mode. These measures present, in one simple figure, a summary of characteristics of an entire group, such as the average sales figures of agents, or the average amount of calls resolved by a customer service agent.

The other category under summary stats is the dispersion, or variance: how much variability exists. One of the most used measures of dispersion is the standard deviation. This reveals how much each individual score or figure in the group is dispersed. For example, a large standard deviation for the average attendance of call center agents means that absenteeism varies greatly from person to person in that group of employees. One key insight provided by Deming and Juran in quality is that variability is seen in everything we do. Performance improvement depends on reducing the variability so that all performers reach the required/desired performance criteria.

Another purpose for statistics is that it allows for the determination of the relationship between two or more events (such as profit and holidays), or scores or items that represent these events. Earlier in this chapter, the importance of synthesis to understand the interdependencies between variables was underscored. In analyzing data, the relationship between one or more items will likely be important. The term used for this relationship in quantitative techniques is *correlation*, which represents the degree to which the items are related and is expressed in terms of a coefficient (ranging from -/+ 0 to 1). A positive correlation between two items means that as one item or score increases, so does the other item or score. For example, high achievement in school might positively correlate with effective note-taking techniques. A negative correlation between two scores (represented by a negative coefficient), on the other hand, means that as one item increases, the other decreases.

One important thing worth mentioning here is that *correlation does not mean causation*. That is, a relationship between two variables does not automatically indicate that a change in one caused a change in the other. One alternate possibility is that a third variable caused a change in the two considered. Again, the evaluator is strongly encourage to look at the data in the context of the entire performance system, accounting for a complete (or as complete as is feasible) list of factors that could have impacted the performance indicators of interest.

Statistics also show how to compare the differences in performance between two groups. When performance improves after an HPI intervention, a likely question is: Is the performance of the group receiving the intervention different than that of the group who did not?

Qualitative data (sometimes called soft data) is also subject to analytical routines. Qualitative observations can be ordered by source and by impact. Checking the frequency of qualitative observations will begin to merge qualitative into quantitative data (sometimes called hard data). Continually reflecting and searching for patterns within the data even while the data collection process is still going on can help evaluators proactively adjust and refocus their data collection to render useful information.

Both qualitative and quantitative data sets should be obtained from valid data sources. Once that is done, you examine the information obtained to make sure it is relevant to each issue or evaluative question in the study. Figure 8.2 shows how hard and soft data may be used to find agreement. It should be noted that an additional reason for using soft data is that sometimes hard data do not exist for some important dimensions, such as organizational image or quality of supervision.

Whatever statistical tools are chosen, the evaluator must be sure that they are the right vehicles to answer the evaluation questions. Different questions call for different analyses, as do different levels of measurement. Use the right tool for the job.

While data analysis focuses on organizing and summarizing information, in your findings, you begin to highlight the most important elements, thereby engaging in the process of turning data (the mean is 18) into information (the average number of items sold per day by the sales clerk in this store is about 18). Your findings begin to personalize and make meaningful the numbers that the analysis rendered, but you are not yet interpreting what that means.

Interpretation attaches meaning to such organized information in order to draw plausible and supportable conclusions. Scriven emphasizes that evaluators must arrive at defensible judgments rather than simply measuring objectives. In this sense, data analysis deals with the facts, while interpretation is related to value judgments. Because this is an innately subjective

Figure 8.2   Using Data

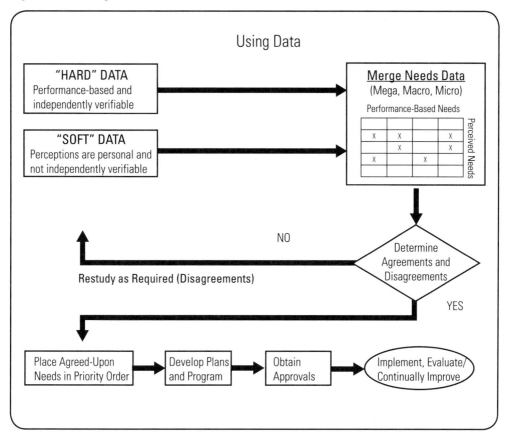

Source: Kaufman, R., 2007.

process, careful attention and effort should be placed on ensuring fairness, openness, and in being as objectively realistic as possible.

Even the most fair and well-meaning evaluators will be biased to some extent; it is the nature of being human. Our perceptions are affected by our past experiences, preferences, values, and habits (such as noticing some details while being unaware of others). Thus, it is helpful to clearly articulate our rationale for the interpretations we make by linking them back to the findings, which are of course based on the data we analyzed. As stated before, this alignment is critical throughout the evaluation process; the data we collected are relevant and valid indicators of the results we want to achieve, which we previously related to important evaluating questions, which we want to answer so that stakeholders can make sound decisions about how to improve performance.

7. Communication of Results and Recommendations. The importance of effective communication cannot be overstated. A rigorous evaluation does not speak for itself. The evaluator may have indeed implemented a flawless evaluation in theory, but it will be worthless if he or she does not communicate the importance and purpose of 1) the evaluation process and associated activities throughout, and 2) the data-supported findings and action that must be taken as a result. If the evaluator cannot move people into action as a result of the evaluation, the main objective has not been met: to create positive (though not necessarily comfortable) change.

Communicating with key stakeholders throughout the evaluation process keeps them aware of what the evaluator is doing and why, which in turn increases the amount of trust they place in the evaluator and her efforts. In addition, it allows stakeholders the opportunity to participate and provide valuable feedback. By the time the final report and debriefing come along, these products will not be seen as something imposed on them, but rather as something that they help created. With this type of buy-in, resistance to the findings will likely be lower.

Things to consider in the communication include medium, format, language, and timing, among others, all of which will be discussed in a later chapter.

Chapter Summary

Change—successful change—is about getting important results and being able to prove that you achieved what you set out to achieve. One of your responsibilities is to demonstrate the evidence. Evaluation compares your needs—What Is and What Should Be—with your accomplishments. Did you accomplish that which you set out to accomplish? Different situations require different kinds of evaluation tools and methods and those are provided in this chapter.

Chapter 9
Performance Dashboards: Monitoring Performance Gaps

What's in This Chapter?

- A step-by-step plan for creating a performance dashboard

- Using dashboards to ensure the capture and monitoring of valid, timely data

- How to decide what data to monitor and ignore

- How leadership can use needs assessment gap information to make decisions

---

Managing and Improving Through Measurement

*What doesn't get measured doesn't get done…*or at least it doesn't get done well. The serious and responsible practice of performance improvement requires the use of data to diagnose performance gaps. It is equally important to track those gaps, over time, both through periodic needs assessments as well as evaluations.

Without accurate and timely performance feedback—provided by ongoing measurement and tracking of performance indicators—it becomes nearly impossible to efficiently and effectively see progress toward closing performance gaps. It becomes equally difficult to make intelligent decisions about what to change, how to change, what to leave alone, and what to abandon altogether. The feedback provided by performance measurement therefore provides a unique and crucial role in the improvement of human and organizational results.

A compass to keep everything on course. Performance measurement provides a compass that keeps an organization on course toward a desired destination, while providing the intelligence to make day-to-day decisions about how to best get there. Performance measurement can, nevertheless, speak both to effectiveness (Was the target destination reached?) and efficiency (Was the destination reached in the most economical way—whether in terms of time, cost, and other resources?).

Performance dashboards can facilitate the continuous tracking of performance measures required for continuously improving performance from needs assessment to evaluation, and everything in between. The following discussion on performance dashboards is based on previous work by Guerra-López (2008; 2010; 2012).

Performance Dashboards

A *performance dashboard* goes by several labels, including performance data systems, executive dashboards, performance measurement systems, automated performance management systems, performance intelligence systems, or automated performance measurement and management systems. Regardless of the label, they are a collective set of measures or metrics used to gauge performance and in turn manage and improve it. They are computerized, often web-based instruments that can support objective and proactive decision making for improving performance. The concept of a dashboard was adopted from automobile dashboards, which provide drivers with critical data that helps them drive and maintain the automobile safely, efficiently, and effectively.

From a global perspective, this system is a multi-criteria instrument for informing decision makers about a variety of different things. For example, it can track current levels of performance, the set of factors (for example, those we explored during causal analysis in chapter 7) for poor or good performance, and the criteria required for improvement in an efficient and timely manner.

Performance dashboards can provide multiple views to multiple levels of users so that each group has access to information that is related to that group's responsibilities. For example, the executive team could have access to Mega- and Macro-level data and only access other levels as desired, while middle management could have ready access to Macro- and Micro-level data most relevant to carrying out their responsibilities. Likewise, lower management, supervisors, and employees could have access to Micro-level data that is required for competently carrying out their responsibilities. However, a strong argument for universal access could also be made, as it better assures that everyone understands not only their own contributions, but the impact and consequences at all other levels. What you want to avoid is overwhelming all users with all data. For daily use, each user should focus on tracking the performance data that is central to his job responsibilities, and the results for which he is accountable, while reviews of the "whole" could be more periodic and in an appropriate team discussion setting.

What users are able to see are usually graphical representations of quantitative data that enable them to detect gaps between optimal and current levels of performance. Depending on the design of the system, root causes can be linked to such indicators, although the complexity of organizations represents a challenge in tracking all possible factors impacting the indicators.

Performance dashboard views can also provide aggregate information, summaries, reports, context, and highlighted exceptions. Some dashboards provide strata for various levels of concerns (for example, high risk, moderate risk, low risk), that can be defined with specific criteria by stakeholders, much like we did for the prioritization of our gaps in chapters 3–6. This also enables users to detect trends more easily, without the use of more sophisticated analysis techniques. Some performance dashboards are configured to offer various plausible courses of action, in part related to potential causes, and the level of risk. Both Beer (1979) and Blenkinsop (1993) write about the benefits of using performance measurement to support strategic objectives and to pinpoint and monitor improvements in performance. Independent studies by Neely (1991) and Grady (1991), as well a joint study by Eccles and Pyburn (1992) the following year, have noted the links between performance measures and strategic goals or critical success factors at the organizational level.

Figure 9.1 illustrates two typical screen views from performance dashboards, which could be based on the important "Vital Signs" of a program, department, or organization, as suggested by Kaufman. The system then acts as a dashboard that allows individuals to safely "drive" their organizational unit (a division, for example) toward their desired destination in the most direct route.

Issues With Performance Dashboards

If measurement systems are to really facilitate the continual improvement process through monitoring and sound decision making, some issues must be addressed. A 2002 article by Santos, Belton, and Howick (2002) points to two key issues that inhibit performance measurement and management systems from reaching their full potential: 1) problems in their design and implementation and 2) problems with the analysis and use of the information produced by the measurements.

Figure 9.1   Dashboard Visual Representations

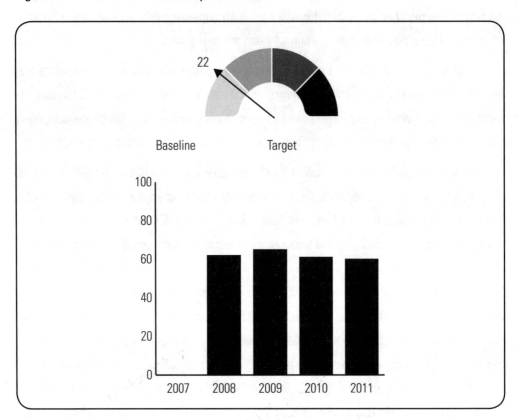

Note: This is an example of a dynamic dashboard. To see an example of a numerical dashboard, as opposed to a graphic view of gauges, see http://www.usdebtclock.org.

Design

Poorly designed measurement systems can compromise their implementation and, in turn, their effectiveness. One important factor for organizations to consider is the selection of an appropriate measurement framework. Some strides have been made to design procedures to identify and group performance measures in a way that makes interpretation more straightforward. However, both a 1999 article by Neely and one from 2000 by Biticci and colleagues recognize that much still has to be done in way of identifying relationships between measures.

While some may recognize the importance of understanding relationships between the various performance measures tracked, organizations continue to design performance dashboards without formally accounting for the interdependencies between the measures, which could ultimately undermine the validity and utility of the information produced by the system.

To address the identification of relationships, in 2000 Suwignjo, Biticci, and Carrie developed quantitative models for performance measurement systems (QMPMS) using cognitive maps, cause-and-effect diagrams, tree diagrams, and the analytic hierarchy process. They describe a technique used to identify factors impacting performance and their relationships, structure them hierarchically, quantify the effect of the factors on performance, and express them quantitatively.

We suggest using Kaufman's Organizational Elements Model and Guerra-López's Impact Evaluation Process as two integrated frameworks for the design of effective performance dashboards that can be used for both continuous needs assessments and evaluations. Moreover, we suggest a customized causal analysis framework, as a secondary element of this design. Together, we believe these three dimensions will help ensure a performance dashboard that is better poised to improve decision making and performance.

Implementation

In addition to design considerations, organizations that are interested in using performance measurement systems must also consider implementation. Poor implementation is a common reason that new organizational initiatives fail. Effective implementation requires careful planning and management of the desired change. Leadership must play an active role in establishing expectations and appropriate consequences, modeling desired behaviors, and motivating those affected. A performance measurement and management system must be seen as one component within an entire performance management system, not as an addition seemingly unrelated to work and management responsibilities. See chapters 7 and 8 for more on the creation, implementation, and management of change.

Analysis and Interpretation

Another set of challenges facing these systems is related to the proper analysis of the data and the use of the information to improve performance. A rigorous analysis must take into account the context of the performance data observed. This includes the many other factors that are actually affecting performance. With the obvious limitations of the human mind and the performance measurement system in accounting for every performance factor, the task is not straightforward.

For instance, one may have to account for the fact that the gains in one performance indicator come at the expense of another performance indicator. If one studies the latter independent of the former, they might draw wrong conclusions, which could lead to poor and costly decisions. Performance improvement professionals often face this situation in conducting needs assessment and analyses, where they limit their search to symptoms and stop before they identify actual performance gaps and root causes. Organizations are dynamic and the design and delivery of change must take that dynamism into account. Dashboards can provide excellent information on what is going on so that managers of change can quickly see what is working and what is not.

Santos, Belton, and Howick point out that many authors (including B.F. Skinner in 1974, and da Silveira and Slack in 2001) have argued that organizations cannot succeed in every single performance indicator and that explicit decisions about tradeoffs must be defined. Hereto, prioritization of indicators, objectives, and gaps (as discussed in previous chapters), is relevant and useful.

These are some of the critical issues to keep in mind when considering performance measurement and management systems and how decision makers actually make decisions about what performance to improve and how. Now we turn our attention to considerations for implementation.

When to Apply

Performance dashboards are particularly useful when organizational leaders are committed to integrating them into their management practices and decisions. These displays are particularly helpful in supporting the processes of clarifying and deploying appropriate resources for meeting organizational objectives and plans, such as in needs assessments, tracking the status and relative effectiveness of various organizational initiatives, and making timely decisions about what to change, what to keep, what to modify, and how. For example, if a top-level executive wants to ensure that everyone within the organization clearly understands the strategy over the next five to 10 years, and wants sound and justifiable leadership decisions that are well aligned with this strategy, she may call for the implementation and use of a performance dashboard as a tool.

Avoiding Pitfalls of Dashboards

However, if those intended users are not "on board" with the idea of using the performance dashboards or they do not receive support on the proper use of the dashboard (for example, if the performance indicators that are most relevant to their area of responsibility and management are not made explicit, and they are not supported in the interpretation of the data or how to "translate" data into useful information and recommendations), the dashboards will likely not be used either consistently or appropriately—or at all.

In most organizations, timing plays an important role in the effectiveness of performance dashboards. Having timely, and in some cases, real-time performance data can save time, costs, and other precious resources that can be lost as a result of waiting for end-of-cycle reports (such as monthly, quarterly, or annual reports). Performance dashboards simplify the process and time required to have access to and use these data.

Performance dashboards will **not** be helpful—in fact could destroy organizational effectiveness—if the wrong measures are being tracked, that is, if irrelevant or generic measures are being tracked independently of important management decisions. They also will not help if intended users do not actually use the information from the systems to support their decision making. Finally, cost is an important consideration. While a useful system will require resources, it is also important to weigh the costs with the potential benefits. The system does not have to be the most expensive and sophisticated for it to work well; it just has to enhance the management function, particularly as it relates to decision making. To accomplish this while not spending exorbitant amounts of resources on a system, you may want to limit the measures and system functions to the most critical.

Performance Dashboard: A Guide

Assessment, Analysis, Design, and Development

Below is a list of critical steps to take when creating performance dashboards:

1. Gain leadership commitment and support for the long-term success of the performance dashboards because, without commitment and resources, you cannot proceed. Agree on the scope and ultimate purpose of the performance dashboards.

2. Identify the best people for the following roles: lead for launching the project, lead for design, lead for implementation, and lead for sustaining the measurement and management system. While you want to have continuity among the various system teams, it is also important to realize the strengths and limitations of each team and leader. Some may be better suited to lead the design of the system, but not be well suited to lead an effective and efficient implementation.

3. Identify strategic, tactical objectives (perhaps from current strategic plan, specifically organizational vision and mission) from those responsible for setting organizational direction. After all, the performance dashboard is supposed to help organizational members accomplish organizational objectives. Not starting with organizational objectives could misalign a system, which will ultimately not deliver on its intended benefits.

4. Identify performance indicators and metrics that must be managed in order to impact organizational objectives and their relationships to one another. Recall that it is imperative that the right measures be tracked. Building a system that houses a seemingly unrelated and trivial list of measures could be overwhelming, demoralizing, and could affect the adoption of the performance dashboards as a legitimate management tool.

5. Identify who is responsible for the various sets of indicators and confirm intended system users and their roles. This will be critical for the design, implementation, and ultimate use of the system. No one knows the measures of a given area of responsibility better than the person responsible for it. Consult with them and this will create buy-in from the start, as well as a more useful and responsive system.

6. As a follow-up to the previous point, consider what questions related to the various set of indicators must be asked and answered to effectively manage them. Each of the performance measures will have specific decision points, so be sure you understand what decisions have to be made and what questions have to be answered so that the system is designed to provide support for making these decisions.

7. Find out where to get these answers (data sources). Knowing where to locate the data is just as important as the data itself. For example, when it's important to track complaints of feedback, some examples of data sources might include daily or weekly sales reports, human resource records, or customers.

8. Set standards or target levels for each indicator to be tracked. In order to determine whether there is a performance gap, you have to have two data points. First, what is the ideal or desired level of performance for that indicator that is identified through consensus building of the relevant stakeholders, industry standards, and the like. Second, we require the actual level of performance of the indicator, which is essentially what we seek to track on a timely basis with the performance dashboard. The difference between these two levels provides us with the performance gaps to be addressed.

9. Determine how to analyze and display these answers. This has to be addressed in the front end, when the system is being designed. Consult with people who are well versed in data analysis to set up system functions that allow users to easily view the data in multiple ways with the push of a button. The simpler it is, the more it will be used.

10. Design and develop a customized schedule for finding these answers (some might be minute-to-minute, hourly, daily, weekly, monthly, quarterly, or annually). Again, consult with those responsible for the different areas of measures to learn the frequency with which the various measures have to be measured and tracked.

11. Partner with information technology (IT) to secure the specific technology appropriate for your organization (you may not want to purchase large software and service packages, but rather create your own customized dashboard).

12. Integrate systems into the overall organizational performance management system. Measurement will be useful to the extent that measurement data is used to manage and improve performance.

13. Design and develop a change creation and management plan that will ensure a smooth transition toward using this tool effectively. Just because the system is available doesn't mean that people will automatically accept it and begin using it as intended. Careful thought about how to manage the integration of this change has to be given at the beginning.

14. The system design should be flexible and continually updated to reflect any relevant changes that will impact results and objectives to be pursued and tracked.

Implementation

Implement a change management plan by:

1. Aligning usage requirements with clear and appropriate consequences.

2. Ensuring all relevant players have access to the data.

3. Track how well users are adapting to systems. You might want to set coaching and feedback sessions with users so that they can bring up any glitches they may have encountered with the usage as well as the technology. This will give the project leaders (or those responsible for coaching and support) the opportunity to help users be more comfortable with the system.

4. Adapt systems based on reliable and feasible feedback.

5. Beware of inconsistent data, analysis, and interpretation, and use mechanisms to identify and resolve inconsistencies.

6. Be sure that implementation is going according to plan; if it is not, ensure your current approach will get you to your desired ends more efficiently and effectively.

7. Keep in mind the limited perspective of performance dashboards, and take all necessary steps to find and use data from other sources when required.

Evaluation and Continual Improvement

1. Continually evaluate to determine whether measures being tracked are still appropriate, up-to-date, and sufficient.

2. Track the usage of the system for its effectiveness. You may want to compare current usage (frequency, in what ways is it being used, what impact usage is having) to expected usage. If you see meaningful gaps, explore the reasons for these gaps so that you come up with plausible alternatives. While the idea is for usage to be up to standards, it may be that current usage is actually more appropriate than what you had initially planned, given what you knew at the time.

3. Track feedback from users as to how to improve the system for their requirements.

4. Track progress toward desired results.

5. Continually update required indicators so that the information used to make decisions is always current, relevant, and reliable.

6. Revise as required. It may be necessary for you to revise the design of the system, or you may have to adjust the way in which it is being used. Stay open to revisions that would enhance the utility and positive impact of the system.

Vital Dashboard Factors

Use a Systemic Perspective

As with everything in an organization, these dashboards must be understood and used from a systemic perspective. Simply implementing this kind of system without aligning it to organizational strategy and management will not render the potential benefits. Consider starting with Mega/ external factors (social, geopolitical, cultural, economic, legal, and so forth) that affect the organization as well as what impact the organization has or could potentially have on these Mega/ external factors. What impact could your performance dashboard have on these factors? How could these factors impact the design, use, and value added of the performance measurement and management system?

Align Expectations With Appropriate Consequences

It is also important to think about the entire performance system and how well the measurement and management systems are aligned to continually deliver desired results that contribute to an efficient and effective organization. One critical element is proper linkage between performance expectations, measures, and consequences or incentives. Effective use of the measurement and management system will in great part depend on the positive consequences—for individual users, teams, and the organization—associated with its use. If well aligned and organized, the measurement and management systems will support continual improvement.

Stakeholder Buy-In

Begin by asking for and obtaining answers about the benefits and threats to each stakeholder group. If you cannot count on having the resources and authority to integrate your system within the organization, no amount of desire to do it will be enough. You must gain the buy-in of not only the leadership, but other stakeholders who could either affect or be affected by the system. Be sure that all those affected by the system or who have influence over the system (note that any organizational member has the capacity to influence the system and the organization, not just top leadership) are well informed of the intent, process, benefits, and challenges of implementing the performance dashboard.

Proper Design

It's worth noting once again that the success of the performance measurement and management hinges on tracking the appropriate sets of indicators, at the appropriate times, for the appropriate reason: managing and improving performance. If the system is not thoughtfully designed with this end in mind, the effort and technology spent on designing the system will be wasted. Again, the system cannot stand on its own. Proper design means aligning the performance dashboard with other performance improvement activities such as coaching, training, and reward systems. In turn, the data from those activities feed back into the measurement system.

Consistent and Appropriate Usage

Just having a system will not automatically result in better management decisions. The system must be consistently and appropriately used if it is going to be helpful. Integrate usage as part of a broader performance management system, especially by clarifying expectations and consequences for usage and non-usage. Also, it will be necessary to train users and other stakeholders on what proper usage is (for example, reviewing the facts, trends, and likely causes before selecting performance improvement solutions), and what proper usage is not (for example, singling anyone out to chastise him or her for sub-par performance).

Balance of Costs and Benefits

Last, it is important to weigh costs against potential benefits. While performance dashboards have the promise of many benefits such as eliminating redundancies, reducing costly mistakes and wasted resources, and the early detection of and response to performance problems, it is important not to lose sight of potential costs. Collecting and organizing data can be time consuming and costly, even with the help of technology. Be sure to focus on functions and activities that will have an acceptable amount of positive return.

Chapter Summary

When designing and implementing change—at any and all levels—it is important to know at all times what is working and what is not. In this chapter we discussed performance dashboards as integral tools for continually improving performance. If well designed, implemented, and used, they provide timely and relevant feedback that can be used for proactive performance improvement actions. They must be based on a systemic perspective and be part of a comprehensive performance management system, in which desired goals are aligned with desirable consequences for performers. For performance dashboards to meet their full potential, a culture of *measurement for motivation and improvement rather than measurement for finger-pointing and punishment* must be designed, modeled, and sustained.

Chapter 10
Gap Assessment Tools

What's in This Chapter?

- How and when to use gap assessment tools

- Collecting data with questionnaires and how to ensure validity

- Tips for effectively presenting data collected from questionnaires

- How to design gap assessment tools to obtain valid and timely data

Assessment Instruments

A useful assessment instrument allows us to answer important questions, and answer them based on research and evidence. An assessment instrument could be well implemented, but if it was poorly designed, it amounts to nothing useful, and perhaps could even be harmful, as it may render unreliable or inaccurate information that could later be erroneously cited as "research data." The utility of data is a function of, among other things, the reliability and validity of the data collection tools (Guerra-López, 2007; 2008). The data collection tools therefore must be the right fit for attaining the required data.

Other important factors to consider when selecting data collection instruments are the relative costs, time, and expertise required to develop and/or obtain them. Once a range of suitable alternatives have been identified based on the type of data required, and their source, the ultimate selection should be based the relative feasibility of each alternative. While a face-to-face interview might be the best choice in terms of the data the evaluator is after on a given project, the sheer number of those to be interviewed might put the time and money required beyond the scope of the project.

Questionnaires

Quick Considerations for Design and Development

One of the most popular data collection tools is the questionnaire. As a general guideline for increasing the usefulness of questionnaires, questions posed can be geared toward informed opinions such as those based on the target group's personal experience, knowledge, background, and vantage point for observation. It is important that questionnaires avoid items that lead the respondent to speculate about the information being requested, nor should a questionnaire be used to confirm or shape a pre-existing bias.

For instance, you would not want to ask in a questionnaire "If you were to buy this car, how would your spouse feel about your decision?" The respondent could only speculate in her answer to this question. You would not want to ask "Do all of the wonderful safety features included with this car make you feel safer?" That is a "leading" question.

Perhaps no questionnaire can be regarded as perfect or ideal for soliciting all the information required, and in fact, most have inherent advantages as well as flaws (Rea and Parker, 1997). However, there are factors, including professional experience and judgment, which may help ensure any advantages and reduce the effects of inherent flaws of questionnaires. In developing the self-assessments included in this book, the authors have striven to overcome many of these challenges.

Another advantage of using questionnaires, such as those provided here, is that they can be completed by respondents at their own convenience and at their own pace. Though a deadline for completion should be given to respondents, they still have sufficient time to carefully reflect, elaborate, and if appropriate, verify their responses. Of course, the drawback here is that mail-out or online questionnaires can require significantly more time to administer than other methods. The sooner you can get a response, the more likely it will be completed. Questionnaires are useful for assessing views, opinions, perceptions, or attitudes about a particular subject.

It is important to note that the findings of a questionnaire reflect reality according to each individual. For that reason, you should triangulate people's perceptions with other forms of data, such as actual performance that can be measured through observations, work products, and documented records. Whatever the data you are after, all methods you select should be focused on answering the "right" question so that useful decisions can be made.

Questionnaires: Not All the Same

Target population characteristics such as culture, language, education, past experiences, and gender, among others, are also essential to consider. Whether written questionnaires, group techniques, interviews, and tests are used, one must understand the impact of these characteristics when deriving questions and methods to collect data from individuals. The words in a question can mean many different things to different people based myriad factors.

In some instances those developing the data collection instruments can unconsciously over-rely on their own experiences and sense of "What Is." Such is the case with questions that include colloquialisms which, although well known to one group of people, are completely unfamiliar to others. The results from these questions are often misleading, as the interpretations of these questions can potentially be as numerous as the respondents.

Similarly, one approach can be appropriate in a given culture, and perhaps not others. For instance, in some cultures, it is considered rude to publicly disagree with the position of others. In such cases, it may be difficult to use a standard group technique to elicit honest responses from a group.

Perhaps one of the most important advantages is that of providing the possibility of anonymity. Questionnaires can be administered in a way such that responses are not traced back to individual respondents. Explicitly communicating this to potential respondents tends to increase the chances for their cooperation on at least two levels: 1) completing the survey to begin with, and 2) being more forthcoming and honest in their responses. However, even if guaranteed anonymity increases response rate, the overall response rate for questionnaires is usually still lower than for other methods.

When responses are low, follow-ups, oversampling, respondent replacements, and non-respondent studies can contribute toward a more representative, random sample, which is critical for generalization of findings. Still, there will usually be some bias in the sample due to self-selection; some people, for their own reasons, might not respond to a questionnaire. But a representative sample is a "must."

There are number of characteristics across which respondents and non-respondents may differ, and thus can impact the findings. You want to know where people agree and where they do not. This is another important issue to acknowledge with interpreting and presenting data collected through questionnaires.

What Data Should Be Collected?

So exactly what data is collected with questionnaires? How does one determine what questions to ask? The fundamental source of information for the items that will be included is the set of results, indicators, and related questions you want answered. The self-assessments in this book are based on the authors' experiences related to defining and delivering organizational success.

The self-assessments included in this book provide a baseline for each area. They have been developed to provide useful information for most organizations. You may be tempted to customize some of the questions or add new questions that address specific concerns that may be unique to your organization. The guides described in chapter 1 can be valuable for tailoring the instruments to your organization and its culture. Just remember to focus on ends (rather than means) and always maintain societal results as your primary guide for making decisions.

The instruments provided are based on key issues to consider in the design, development, and/or selection of useful questionnaires. The important variables, considered in the items in this book, may be reviewed in Guerra-López (2007).[1]

Questionnaire Structure

Respondents are not only sensitive to the language used in each question, but also the order in which these questions are asked. Keep in mind that each question can become the context for the next. Thus, poorly structured questionnaires can not only confuse the respondents and cause them to provide inaccurate responses, but may also lead them to abandon the questionnaire altogether.

A well-structured questionnaire should begin with straightforward yet interesting questions so as to motivate the respondent to continue. As with any relationship, it takes time for an individual to feel comfortable with sharing sensitive information, therefore sensitive items should be saved for later on in the questionnaire. Questions that focus on the same specific issue should be presented together, so as to maximize the respondent's reflection and recall. One way for both the questionnaire designer and the respondent is to cluster specific items around different categories.

Simplicity is key. Nobody wants to complete a long and complicated questionnaire. The questionnaire should include exactly what is required. Nothing more, nothing less. Only relevant

---

1. For a more advanced analysis of developing and testing items with a questionnaire, see DeVellis (2003) *Scale Development: Theory and Applications*.

indicators should form the basis of a questionnaire. While there may be plenty of interesting information that could be collected through the questionnaire, if it is not central to the indicators being investigated, it will only be a distraction—both for the evaluators and the respondent.

In considering the length of the questionnaire, the questionnaire crafter should not only think about the actual length of the questionnaire, but the length of time the respondent will invest in completing it. As a general rule, the entire questionnaire should take no more than 30 minutes to complete, and ideally, about half that long.

Suggested Data Analysis Approaches

This section focuses on the suggested analysis approach specifically for the instruments, or the type of instruments using the same dual measurement scales, presented in this book. Patterns are of particular importance. Review the responses (by you and/or others if that is your choice) and note any patterns that emerge. Gaps between What Is and What Should Be for each section and item should be estimated, with those gaps over 1.5 points meriting special attention. You might also consider prioritizing some of these gaps based on magnitude, importance, urgency, or other prioritization criteria that might be particularly relevant to you and your organization. Below are four analysis criteria that are worth exploring, but you may come up with others that are particularly meaningful for you and your organization.

Analysis One: Discrepancy

For each question of the self-assessment a gap analysis should be performed by subtracting the value assigned to the WI column from the value assigned to the WSB column (see Figure 10.1). The results of this analysis will identify discrepancies between the current and desired performance for each variable associated with the e-learning system. The size of the gap can provide valuable information in determining the perceived acuteness of the need or the extent to which opportunities can be capitalized upon.

Figure 10.1 is an example of a two response column format from an online self-assessment of What Is and What Should Be.

The results of this analysis are, however, necessary rather than sufficient for quality decision making. Alone they only provide isolated values (data points) that have to be put into context through their relationships with other analyses described below.

Figure 10.1   Two Response Column Format From an Online Self-Assessment

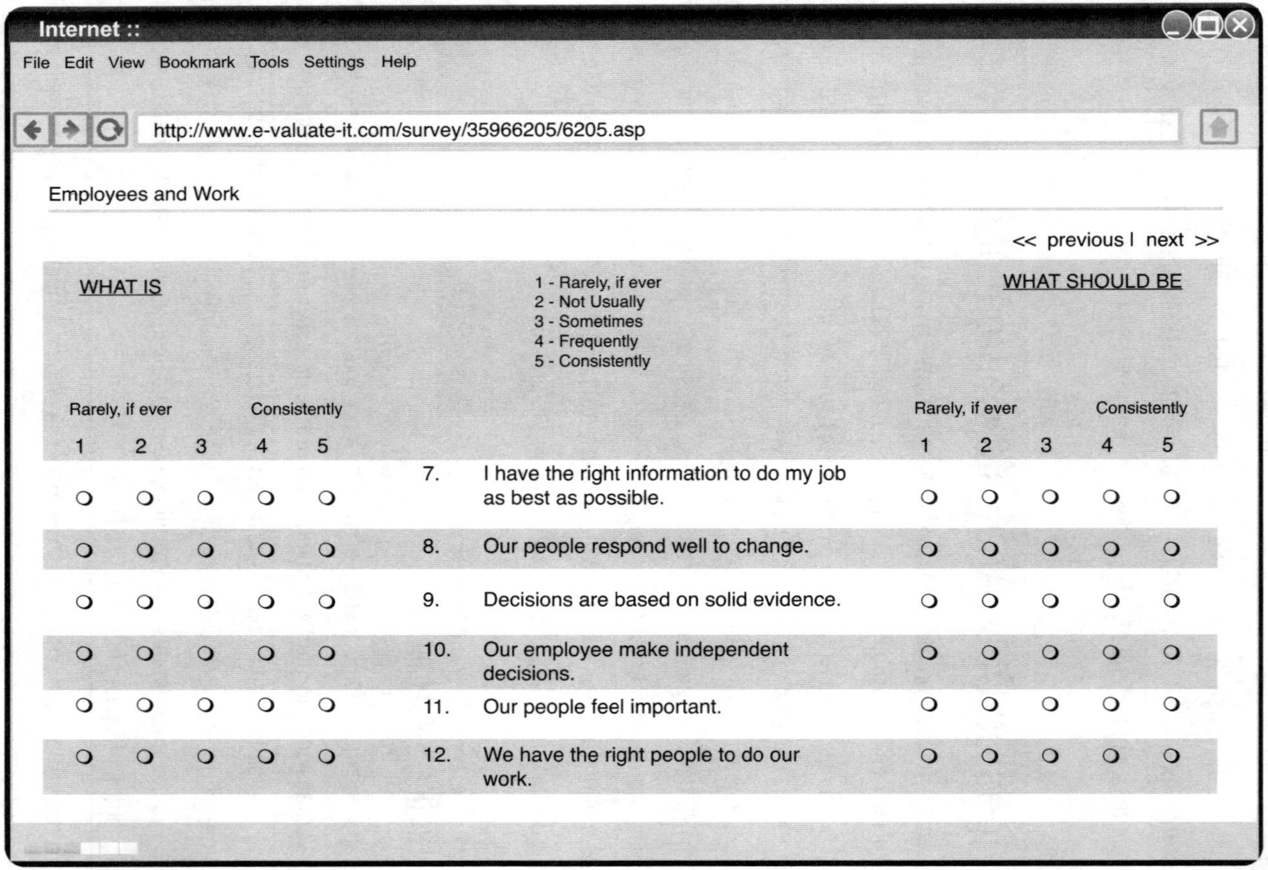

Internet ::

File Edit View Bookmark Tools Settings Help

http://www.e-valuate-it.com/survey/35966205/6205.asp

Employees and Work

<< previous I next >>

1 - Rarely, if ever
2 - Not Usually
3 - Sometimes
4 - Frequently
5 - Consistently

WHAT IS

	Rarely, if ever				Consistently
	1	2	3	4	5

WHAT SHOULD BE

	Rarely, if ever				Consistently
	1	2	3	4	5

7. I have the right information to do my job as best as possible.

8. Our people respond well to change.

9. Decisions are based on solid evidence.

10. Our employee make independent decisions.

11. Our people feel important.

12. We have the right people to do our work.

Analysis Two: Direction

For each question the positive or negative value of the gap should be identified to differentiate needs (when WSB is greater than WI) from opportunities (when WI is greater than WSB).

- Positive discrepancies between WSB and WI (for example, WSB = 5, WI = 3, Gap = 3) identifies a *need*.

- Negative discrepancies between WSB and WI (for example, WSB = 3, WI = 4, Gap = -1) identifies an *opportunity*.

The distinction of needs and opportunities provides a context for discrepancy data, which by itself only illustrates the size of the gap between What Should Be and What Is. Based on the direction of the discrepancy, decision makers can consider which gaps illustrate needs that have the potential to be addressed through organizational efforts, and which identify opportunities that the organization may want to leverage (or maintain) in order to ensure future success.

A general format for questions that ask the respondent to rate items on What Is and What Should Be is shown in Figure 10.2; the figure shows the discrepancy format and provides an example of questions relating to Mega.

Analysis Three: Position

The position analysis illustrates the relative importance or priority of discrepancies from the perspective of the respondents. While many gaps between What Should Be and What Is may have equivalent discrepancies and be in the same direction, the position of the discrepancy on the Likert scale of the instrument can demonstrate the relative priority of the discrepancy in relation to other gaps.

For example, two needs may be identified with a discrepancy of +3, but one need illustrated a gap between WSB = 5 and WI = 2 while the other illustrated WSB = 3 and WI = 0. As a result, the interpretation of these discrepancies in relation to one another would indicate a perceived prioritization of the initial need over the other. This information can be valuable in selecting which discrepancies are addressed when resources are limited.

Together, the three analyzes (discrepancy, direction, and position) can offer valuable data for identifying, prioritizing, and selecting performance improvement efforts related to the complete e-learning system.

Figure 10.2   Example of a Discrepancy Format

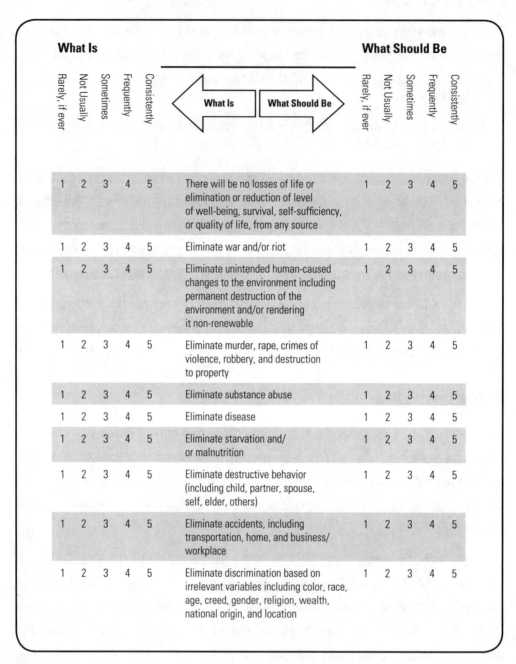

Source: Kaufman, R., and Guerra-López, I., 2008.

Analysis Four: Demographic Differences (Optional)

Organizations may want to view the results of the self-assessment based on demographic differences (such as division, location, position type, years of experience). Analysis of the results of the self-assessment can be reviewed by demographic variables if items related to the desired categories are added to the instrument. If your organization has collected data regarding the demographics of those completing the self-assessment, the analysis for discrepancy, direction, and position should be completed for each demographic on a section, subsection, or item basis depending on the level of information required for decision making.

Displaying Response Data

A visual representation such as a matrix or a bar chart for illustrating the results is suggested. If you implement this instrument for a group of people, you may also want to indicate the percentage of people who indicated each response option, giving you insight into where the majority of the respondents' perceptions lie. Additionally, you can plot the gaps between the median scores for What Is and What Should Be. While using means, or mathematical averages, is actually not a proper manipulation of scores, it can also be presented, along with its gaps, as a source of comparison for those who are used to interpreting data in that fashion (see Figures 10.3 and 10.4). By displaying your results this way, you and your associates can quickly scan and see both gaps and patterns.

Interpretation and Required Action

With the data analyzed, and patterns apparent, you will want to extrapolate what this all means. Depending on who is involved, the data could mean various things to various people. Not all interpretations are equally viable. Be sure to consider all viable interpretations, verifying these with additional relevant and valid information.

You may also want to collect information on why these gaps exist (via a causal or SWOT analysis), so that the solutions and courses of action you consider have a high probability of closing those gaps, and in turn, yield the consequences you want and require.

Figure 10.3   Gap Magnitude by Question

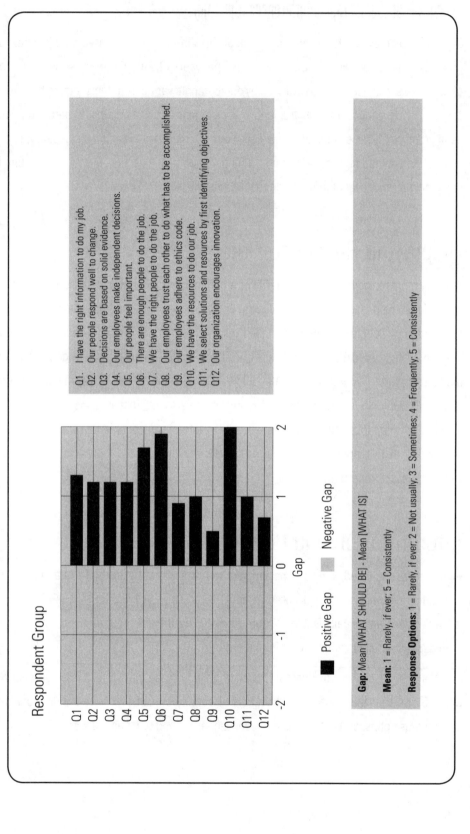

Figure 10.4   Gap Range by Question

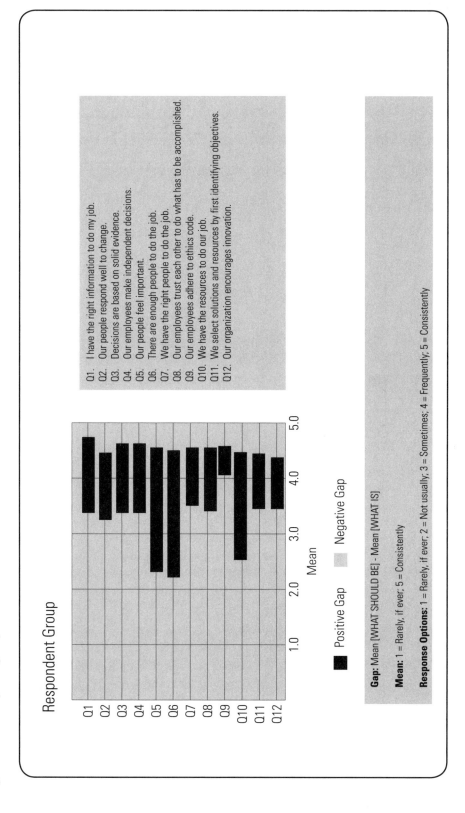

Respondent Group

Q1. I have the right information to do my job.
Q2. Our people respond well to change.
Q3. Decisions are based on solid evidence.
Q4. Our employees make independent decisions.
Q5. Our people feel important.
Q6. There are enough people to do the job.
Q7. We have the right people to do the job.
Q8. Our employees trust each other to do what has to be accomplished.
Q9. Our employees adhere to ethics code.
Q10. We have the resources to do our job.
Q11. We select solutions and resources by first identifying objectives.
Q12. Our organization encourages innovation.

Mean

■ Positive Gap   Negative Gap

Gap: Mean [WHAT SHOULD BE] - Mean [WHAT IS]

Mean: 1 = Rarely, if ever; 5 = Consistently

Response Options: 1 = Rarely, if ever; 2 = Not usually; 3 = Sometimes; 4 = Frequently; 5 = Consistently

Chapter Summary

Not all data collection instruments are created equal. We identified the characteristics of several so you can match an instrument with the questions to which you require answers. The most useful often include asking What Is and What Should Be for questions that are results related.

Chapter 11
Tool Kit

What's in This Chapter?

• This chapter provides exercises and job aids that you can use to ensure that you and your planning partners are clear about many of the distinctions in this book as well as provide some guidance for conducting evidence-based needs assessments.

1. New Realities Facing All Organizations—Which Ones Apply to You and Your Organization

Below is a list of "new realities." Identify which ones are important for you to be successful with your needs assessments and organizational improvement.

New Reality	Importance for Your Organization
If you embrace the past you cannot produce the future.	
You can't solve today's problems with the same paradigms and approaches that created them.	
There are two bottom lines for any organization: societal and conventional.	
Reality is not divided into organizations, laws, rules, policies, departments, sections, or physical boundaries.	
If you can't predict the future, create it (Drucker).	
It is sometimes easier to kill an organization than to change it (Tom Peters).	
Useful change has to add value to all stakeholders.	
Fix the problem not the blame.	
Don't be the best of the best, be the only one that does what you do (Jerry Garcia).	

Continued on next page.

Continued from previous page.

New Reality	Importance for Your Organization
Incrementalism is like pulling an impacted wisdom tooth slowly.	
Operate as if you intend to put your own organization out of business through success. Pursue perfection.	
The new organizational structure is one of networks and not of hierarchies.	
The resistance to a new idea increases by the square of its importance (Bertrand Russell).	
A problem doesn't cease to exist simply because one chooses to ignore it.	
Everyone is entitled to their own opinion but not to their own data.	
You can make money with people who don't have any (Prahalad).	
Ask "If my organization is the solution, what's the problem?"	
Our world changes and is changeable.	

2. Means and Ends

Following is an exercise that will help you reflect on your understanding of the critical distinction between ends and means. Put a check mark next to each item to identify them as either an end or a mean. Then, check your answers on the following page.

	End	Means
Learning problem solving		
Looking for a job		
Having positive self-esteem		
Do a training needs assessment		
Downsizing		
Evaluating		
College graduate		
Survival		
Six Sigma		
Re-engineering		
Assessing needs		
Training		
Continual improvement		
Team building		
Loving		

Now check your answers:

	End	Means
Learning problem solving		X
Looking for a job		X
Having positive self-esteem	X	
Do a training needs assessment		X
Downsizing		X
Evaluating		X
College graduate	X	
Survival	X	
Six Sigma		X
Re-engineering		X
Assessing needs		X
Training		X
Continual improvement		X
Team building		X
Loving		X

3. Job Aid for Writing Measurable Objectives

Useful Objectives

```
        ┌──────────┐
        │  Start   │
        └────┬─────┘
             │         ┌─────────────┐
             │         │   Revise    │
             ▼         └─────────────┘
         ╱───────╲         ▲
        ╱ Does it ╲   No   │
       ╱  target   ╲───────┘
       ╲ an end?   ╱
        ╲─────────╱
             │ Yes
             ▼
         ╱───────╲
        ╱ Does it ╲   No
       ╱ have      ╲──────────┘
       ╲ rigorous  ╱
        ╲criteria?╱
         ╲───────╱
             │ Yes
             ▼
        ┌──────────┐
        │  Good!   │
        └──────────┘
```

4. Relating Goals and Objectives

Where are you headed and how will you know when you have arrived?

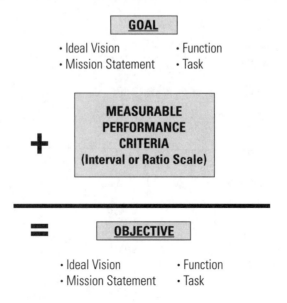

GOAL

- Ideal Vision   - Function
- Mission Statement   - Task

+   **MEASURABLE PERFORMANCE CRITERIA (Interval or Ratio Scale)**

=   **OBJECTIVE**

- Ideal Vision   - Function
- Mission Statement   - Task

5.   Four Scales of Measurement

Name of Scale of Measurement	Label for the Scale	What Each Scale Measures
Nominal	Goal, aim, purpose	Name or label, such as Ingrid or Charles, or Tuesday
Ordinal	Goal, aim, purpose	Greater than, less than, equal to
Interval	Objective	Equal scale distance with an arbitrary zero point, such as temperature in $°F$ or $°C$
Ratio	Objective	Equal scale distance with a known zero point, such as K

If you can name something, you are measuring it.

6.   Objectives: Good and Poor

Following is an exercise that will help you reflect on the difference between good and poor objectives by identifying them as measurable or not. Fill in the chart below and then check your answers on the following page.

Possible Objective	Measurable on an Interval or Ratio Scale	Not Measurable on an Interval or Ratio Scale
Show a profit each and every year.		
Improve productivity.		
Increase effectiveness.		
Reduce errors by at least 5% each month for a year.		
Train salespersons before the end of the year.		
Eliminate fatalities within one year.		
Use Six Sigma in all of our facilities starting next month.		
Evaluate all employees at least once per year and report all results to HR within 10 days.		
Reduce theft.		
Hire competent people.		
Be ranked in the upper 5% of all competing organizations on or before January 1.		

Let's compare results:

Possible Objective	Measurable on an Interval or Ratio Scale	Not Measurable on an Interval or Ratio Scale
Show a profit each and every year.	X	
Improve productivity.		X
Increase effectiveness.		X
Reduce errors by at least 5% each month for a year.	X	
Train salespersons before the end of the year.		X
Eliminate fatalities within one year.	X	
Use Six Sigma in all of our facilities starting next month.		X
Evaluate all employees at least once per year and report all results to HR within 10 days.		X
Reduce theft.		X
Hire competent people.		X
Be ranked in the upper 5% of all competing organizations on or before January 1.	X	

7. Needs Assessment Selection Algorithm

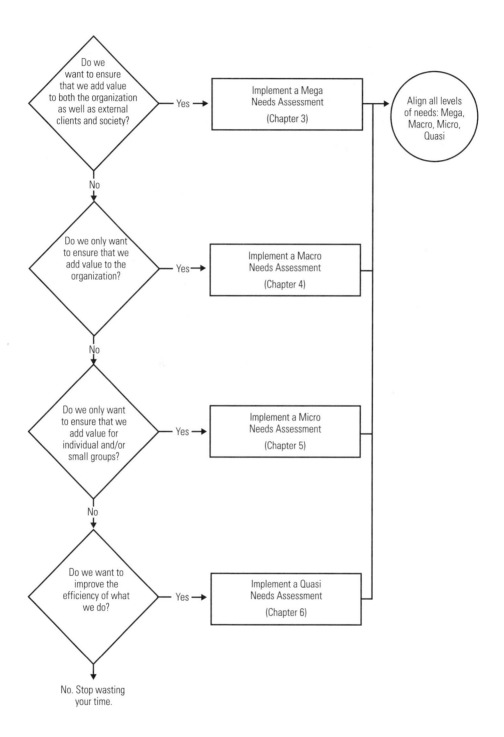

8. Six Critical Success Factors for Useful Strategic Thinking and Planning

1. DON'T ASSUME THAT WHAT WORKED IN THE PAST WILL WORK NOW. GET OUT OF YOUR COMFORT ZONE AND BE OPEN TO CHANGE.

2. USE AN IDEAL VISION AS THE UNDERLYING BASIS FOR PLANNING (don't be limited to your organization).

3. DIFFERENTIATE BETWEEN ENDS AND MEANS (focus on what before how).

4. PREPARE OBJECTIVES—INCLUDING IDEAL VISION AND MISSION OBJECTIVES—WHICH HAVE MEASURES OF HOW YOU WILL KNOW WHEN YOU HAVE ARRIVED (mission statement plus success criteria).

5. USE ALL THREE LEVELS OF PLANNING AND RESULTS (Mega/Outcomes, Macro/Outputs, and Micro/Products).

6. DEFINE "NEED" AS A GAP IN RESULTS (not as insufficient levels of resources, means, or methods).

9.   Job Aid for Needs Assessments: Ensuring a Mega-Focus

Ensuring an Objective Links to All 3 Levels of Results

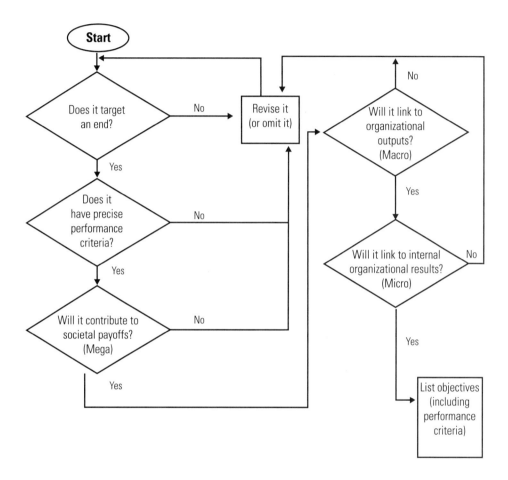

10. Linking and Aligning All Three Organizational Levels in Needs Assessment

Linking and Overlap of Levels of Planning and Doing

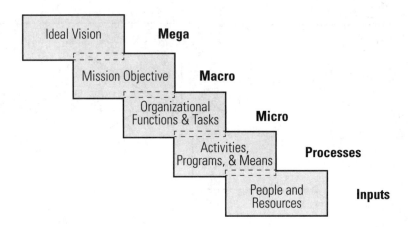

11. A Needs Assessment Summary Format

Current Results	Possible Means	Required Results	Related Ideal Vision Element	Needs Level Focus		
				Mega	Macro	Micro

12. The Basic Ideal Vision and Vital Signs

Basic Ideal Vision:
The world we want to help create for the future generations.

- There will be no losses of life nor elimination or reduction of levels of well-being, survival, self-sufficiency, quality of life, from any source including (but not limited to):

    - war and/or riot and/or terrorism and/or civil unrest

    - unintended human-caused changes to the environment including permanent destruction of the environment and/or rendering it non-renewable

    - murder, rape, crimes of violence, robbery, or destruction of property

    - substance abuse

    - disease

    - starvation and/or malnutrition

    - destructive behavior (including child, partner, spouse, self, elder, other)

    - accidents, including transportation, home, and business/workplace

    - discrimination based on irrelevant variables including color, race, age, creed, gender, religion, wealth, national origin, or location.

- Poverty will not exist, and every woman and man will earn as least as much as it costs them to live unless they are progressing toward being self-sufficient and self-reliant. No adult will be under the care, custody, or control of another person, agency, or substance: Adult citizens will be self-sufficient and self-reliant as minimally indicated by their consumption being equal to or less than their production.

13. Applying the Ideal Vision and Vital Signs

Following are three application exercises that will structure the questions an organization must ask and answer in order to provide the basis for collecting valid data for useful leadership decisions. This may help you facilitate the preliminary discussion with your needs assessment and planning partners.

Chapter 11

Are an Ideal Vision and related vital signs important for the organization? For each item select your response.

The Ideal Vision	Important for My Organization and Our Community or Shared World	It Will Have No Impact on My Organization, Community, or Shared World
There will be no losses of life, elimination or reduction of levels of well-being, survival, self-sufficiency, or quality of life from any source.	?	?

If the response was that the Ideal Vision and vital signs are important for one's organization, then move ahead. If not, seriously question if your organization has a future if it is not making our world safe as well as all individual and external stakeholders.

Vital signs for achieving the Ideal Vision. Identify the gaps between current results and required results for these elements that are important for you and your organization to reduce or eliminate.

Vital Signs			
First Level: Basic Survival for All People	Yes, Directly	Yes, With Other Partners	Someone Else's Problem/No Problem
Zero pollution—no permanent destruction of our environment			
No deaths or permanent disabilities from what is delivered			
No starvation and/or malnutrition resulting in death or incapacity			
No partner or spouse abuse resulting in death or incapacitating physical or psychological damage			
No disease or disabilities resulting in death or incapacity			
No substance abuse resulting in death or incapacity			
No murder, rape, crimes of violence, robbery, fraud, or destruction of property			
No war, riot, terrorism, or civil unrest resulting in death or incapacity of individuals or groups			
No accidents resulting in death or incapacity			

Second Level: Organizational Survival			
Continued funding based on measurable positive return-on-investment			
No successful lawsuits against the organization for defecting or inappropriate units or services			
Programs, projects, activities, and operations meet all performance objectives and do not violate first tier requirements			

Selecting and ranking vital signs. Identify gaps in results for those variables that you have selected and rank their importance or criticality for you, your organization, and your external clients. Data to support this should be both valid and measurable on an interval or ratio scale.[1]

Vital Signs	Data	Data	Rank
First Level: Basic Survival for All people	**Current Results and Consequences**	**Desired Results and Consequences**	**Importance/ Criticality Rank for Each From 1 (Vital) to 5 (Not Immediate)**
Zero pollution—no permanent destruction of our environment			
No deaths or permanent disabilities from what is delivered			
No starvation and/or malnutrition resulting in death or incapacity			
No partner or spouse abuse resulting in death or incapacitating physical or psychological damage			
No disease or disabilities resulting in death or incapacity			

Continued on next page.

1. There are four scales of measurement: nominal/naming, ordinal/rank-order, interval/equal scale distances with arbitrary zero point, and ratio/ equal scale distances and known zero point (Stevens, 1951; Kaufman, 1972). Objectives are defined as being measurable on an interval or ordinal scale. Purposes or intents are measurable on a nominal or ordinal scale. We recommend that all statements of purpose be objectives as defined here.

Continued from previous page.

Vital Signs	Data	Data	Rank
First Level: Basic Survival for All people	**Current Results and Consequences**	**Desired Results and Consequences**	**Importance/ Criticality Rank for Each From 1 (Vital) to 5 (Not Immediate)**
No substance abuse resulting in death or incapacity			
No murder, rape, crimes of violence, robbery, fraud, or destruction of property			
No war, riot, terrorism, or civil unrest resulting in death or incapacity of individuals or groups			
No accidents resulting in death or incapacity			
Second Level: Organizational Survival			
Continued funding or profits based on measurable positive return-on-investment			
No successful lawsuits against the organization for defecting or inappropriate units or services			
Programs, projects, activities, and operations meet all performance objectives and do not violate first tier requirements			

14. Exercise for Coming to Agreement on a Mega/Societal Focus

When deciding to use Mega and the Ideal Vision, you might want to come to agreement on the importance of including and linking all levels. Here are some questions to consider.

Level of planning and organizational commitment:

Level of planning and type of results	My organization must address formally
Mega/Outcomes	Yes/No
Macro/Outputs	Yes/No
Micro/Products	Yes/No
Processes	Yes/No
Input	Yes/No
Continual Improvement (evaluation)	Yes/No
Level of planning and type of results	**My organization currently addresses formally**
Mega/Outcomes	Yes/No
Macro/Outputs	Yes/No
Micro/Products	Yes/No
Processes	Yes/No
Input	Yes/No
Continual Improvement (evaluation)	Yes/No

Next, by comparing what your organization should formally address to what it is currently formally addressing, you can identify the gaps between What Is and What Should Be. Consider the risks and gains for not including all of the organizational elements.

15. Organizational Questions to Be Asked and Answered

Based on the questions that all organizations must ask and answer, please respond to the following as a small group:

- Which of the questions do you think your organization and any of your internal and external clients can afford to NOT address formally? (This means without identifying and dealing with each in measurable performance terms.)

Level of Planning and Type of Results	Can Afford to Not Address Formally and Rigorously	Must Address Formally and Rigorously
Mega/Outcomes		
Macro/Outputs		
Micro/Products		
Processes		
Inputs		
Continuous Improvement		

- Which of the questions do you believe your organization and any of its internal and external clients currently do and do not formally and completely address in measurable performance terms?

- What are the risks for starting at the Mega level? What are the risks for NOT starting at the Mega level?

- In what ways are you adding value to your organization? To your external clients? To our community and society? What could you be doing and contributing? How do you know if you are adding value?

16. Data Collection Considerations

Things to Consider in Developing a Needs Assessment Questionnaire

- Make certain that the questions are about results, not about processes or inputs.

- Ask about perceptions of gaps in results for both dimensions—what is and what should be.

- Ask questions about the three levels of results-referenced needs:

  - external contributions

  - organizational contributions

  - building-block results (products).

- Have evidence of appropriate validity and reliability of the questions and the sample.

- Make the questionnaire long enough to get reliable responses, but short enough that people will actually respond.

- Use an approach that makes it clear to respondents exactly what is wanted. People usually don't want to write long answers, so a checklist or multiple-choice format will reduce their burden while making the questionnaire easier to score.

- Don't ask questions that reveal, directly or indirectly, a bias. Don't use the data-collection vehicle to set up the responses you really want.

- Ask several questions about each dimension or issue. Ask about each concern in different ways, to increase the reliability of responses. Basing any decision on answers to one question is risky.

- Try out the data-collection instrument on a sample group to identify problems in meaning, coverage, and scorability. Revise it as required. (This step is the same as the sixth step in the problem-solving model, continuous improvement.)

Tips for Collecting Performance Data

- Make certain the data collected relate to important questions for which you want answers.

- Assure yourself that the data are collected correctly and that the methods used for gathering it and reporting it are free of any bias.

- Assure yourself that the data are based upon enough observations to make them reliable, not a one-shot happening.

- Make certain that the data can be independently verified and cross-checked.

17.   What Is and What Is Not a Needs Assessment?

Fuzzy Worldwide Industries: A Hypothetical Needs Assessment Case Study

Here is a hypothetical example of the results of a needs assessment done by Fuzzy Worldwide Industries. Answer the questions following the summary.

Need Assessment Summary

1.   We have to have supervisors managing with vision.

2.   We need to be world class.

3.   We have to be competitive.

4.   We need more executive training.

5.   We need to cut down on training time.

6.   A need exists to make quality our first priority.

7.   We must all work together.

8.   We must increase our production by 18 percent.

9.   There must be no injuries or deaths from what we deliver.

10. We must make a profit each year and every year.

11. We must not pollute the environment, bringing harm to living things.

12. We need to use performance technology.

- Examine the needs assessment and identify which elements of it:
  - identify a need as a gap in results
  - identify a Quasi need: a need as a gap in methods or a gap in resources.
- For each need identified, classify it as:
  - Mega/Outcomes-related
  - Macro/Outputs-related
  - Micro/Products-related (Note the needs listed for each results level.)
  - Anything missing?

- For each Quasi need, ask "If I did or delivered this, what result would I get?" Keep asking that question until you have identified needs at the three levels of results. List them.

- Using the Needs Assessment Self-Assessment (previous), review an existing needs assessment and identify if it is likely to be useful and appropriate. If the reviewed needs assessment does not meet the basic criteria, what changes to it should be made?

Let's compare answers.

1. *We have to have supervisors managing with vision.*

This is a means (Process). It states nothing about what results and payoffs there will be from "managing with vision" nor does it state what the vision will be.

2. *We need to be world class.*

This aspiration never defines what "world class" is or how we would measure it. It also does not state what the results and payoffs will be from being "world class." This does not relate to a need but is an intention, and a fuzzy one at that.

3. *We have to be competitive.*

This aspiration never defines what "competitive" is or how we would measure it. It also does not state what the results and payoffs will be from being competitive. This does not relate to a need but is an intention, and—like #2—another fuzzy one.

4. *We need more executive training.*

This is a means. Your first clue that it is the use of "need" as a verb, and that dumps one into means without defining the ends to be accomplished. In this case, what gap in results would be closed by "more executive training"? What gap in results would this deliver at the Mega, Macro, and Micro levels?

5. *We need to cut down on training time.*

This is also a means. Your first clue again is the use of "need" as a verb, and that dumps one into means without defining the ends to be accomplished. In this case, what gap in results would be closed by "cutting down on training time"? What gap in results would this deliver at the Mega, Macro, and Micro levels?

6. *We need to make quality our first priority.*

Again, this is a means. Your clue is again the use of "need" as a verb, limiting means without defining the ends to be accomplished. In this case, what gap in results would be closed by "making quality our first priority"? What is "quality" and how do we measure it? What gap in results would this deliver at the Mega, Macro, and Micro levels?

7. *We must all work together.*

This is also a means. In this case, what gap in results would be closed by "working together"? What gap in results would "working together" deliver at the Mega, Macro, and Micro levels?

8. *We must increase our production by 18 percent.*

At last a result, at the Micro level. If it were stated as a "need"—a gap between current results and desired ones—it might be stated as: "Current production is at x and we will increase it to at least y, an increase of production of at least 18 percent."

9. *There must be no injuries or deaths from what we deliver.*

This will deliver results at the Mega level. If stated as a need, it might read: "Last year there were three disabling injuries and one death from our Outputs. Next year and following there will be no disabling injuries and no deaths from our Outputs."

10. *We must make a profit each and every year.*

This will deliver results at the Mega level, to the extent to which profit is earned without bringing harm to anyone or the environment. Profit over time is an indicator of a Mega-level contribution. If stated as a need, it might read: "Last year we had a loss of $2.23 million. Next year—and for following years—we will increase our profits by at least 5 percent."

11. *We must not pollute the environment, bringing harm to living things.*

This will deliver results at the Mega level, to the extent to which what our organization does and delivers does not bring harm to the environment and living things; they are "good neighbors." If stated as a need, it might read: "Last year we had two spills cited by the environmental council for being toxic and destructive. Next year—and for following years—we will have no incidents causing toxic damage or other kinds of destruction."

12. We need to use performance technology.

"Performance technology" is a means, even though it can be a very powerful means. Ask "If we were successful at using performance technology, what would the results of that be?"

Also, notice that none of Fuzzy Worldwide Industries' "needs" were stated as gaps in results. This is a common mistake, and one you can avoid. Also, notice how many times "need" was used as a verb ("we 'need' to use performance technology") and thus moving anything the organization used, does, and delivers toward a focus on solutions rather than on results and value added.

18. A Decision Table for Agreeing on Mega in Needs Assessment and Planning

Provide each person involved in your needs assessment and planning with each question in order. Require everyone—the clients and you as the planner—to sign or initial each item. If anyone has any questions about the meaning of an item, just tell him to initial under "no."

Usually, by the fourth or fifth question, those who said "no" previously, will now start getting the picture. This is a very effective tool for getting agreement on Mega and for aligning everything that is issued, done, produced, and delivered, as well as the external impact and payoffs.

		Commitment			
		Clients		Planners	
		Y	N	Y	N
1.	The total organization will contribute to clients' and societal survival, health, and well-being.				
2.	The total organization will contribute to clients' and societal quality of life.				
3.	Clients' and societal survival, health, and well-being will be part of the organization's and each of its facilities' mission objectives.				
4.	Each organizational operation function will have objectives which contribute to #1, #2, and #3.				
5.	Each job/task will have objectives which contribute to #1, #2,#3, and #4.				
6.	A need assessment will identify and document any gaps in results at the operational level of #1, #2, #3, #4, and #5.				
7.	Human resources/training and/or operations requirements will be based on the needs identified and selected in step #6.				
8.	The results of #6 may recommend non-HRD/training interventions.				
9.	Evaluation and continual improvement will compare results with objectives for #1, #2, #3, #4, and #5.				

19. Assessing Your Organization's Culture Concerning Needs Assessment

How to Complete This Assessment

There are two dimensions to this assessment instrument that allow you to compare the current status of your organization with a preferred status: 1) What Is and 2) What Should Be with regards to needs assessment. This follows the definition of a need as a gap between current results and desired or required results; between What Is and What Should Be.

In the first column (left side), indicate how you see your organization currently operating. In the second column (right side), indicate how you feel your organization should be operating. For each item, think of the phrase: "In our organization, from my experience…" as you consider the current and preferred states of the organization. If there are items about which you are uncertain, give your best response.

Items 1-6 and 12-15 let you and your partners identify gaps between What Is and What Should Be for a results- and evidence-based use of needs assessments.

Items 7-8 reveals if conventional yet counterproductive approaches to needs assessment exist. Gaps here, ideally, are small for both What Is and What Should Be.

Items 9-11 reveal possible problems with the organizational culture, such as not having the human resources to perform useful results-based needs assessments.

This exercise is useful for getting agreement among your partners on what it takes to do a useful needs assessment.

What Is					Needs Assessment	What Should Be				
1 – Rarely, if ever	2 – Not Usually	3 – Sometimes	4 – Frequently	5 – Consistently	1 – Rarely, if ever 2 – Not Usually 3 – Sometimes 4 – Frequently 5 – Consistently	1 – Rarely, if ever	2 – Not Usually	3 – Sometimes	4 – Frequently	5 – Consistently
1	2	3	4	5	1. We formally plan.	1	2	3	4	5
1	2	3	4	5	2. We do needs assessments.	1	2	3	4	5
1	2	3	4	5	3. Needs assessments are valued in our organization.	1	2	3	4	5
1	2	3	4	5	4. We use the data from needs assessments to decide what to do and accomplish.	1	2	3	4	5
1	2	3	4	5	5. Our needs assessment examines the gaps between obtained results and our predetermined objectives.	1	2	3	4	5
1	2	3	4	5	6. Needs assessments are results focused.	1	2	3	4	5
1	2	3	4	5	7. Needs assessments are activities focused.	1	2	3	4	5
1	2	3	4	5	8. We do "training needs assessments."	1	2	3	4	5
1	2	3	4	5	9. The organization skips formal needs assessments because of time restraints.	1	2	3	4	5
1	2	3	4	5	10. The organization skips formal needs assessments because of lack of needs assessment capabilities.	1	2	3	4	5
1	2	3	4	5	11. The organization skips formal needs assessments because of not knowing how to interpret needs assessment data.	1	2	3	4	5
1	2	3	4	5	12. Management is focused on results accomplished (rather than processes and activities engaged in) when it requests or approves a needs assessment.	1	2	3	4	5
1	2	3	4	5	13. The organization's culture is focused on results.	1	2	3	4	5
1	2	3	4	5	14. Needs assessment is seen as comparing current results against those results that should be accomplished.	1	2	3	4	5
1	2	3	4	5	15. Needs assessments are done for strategic planning.	1	2	3	4	5

Source: Kaufman, R., and Guerra-López, I., 2008.

References

Beer, S. (1979). *The Heart of Enterprise.* Hoboken, NJ: John Wiley & Sons.

Bernardez, M. (2005). Achieving Business Success by Developing Clients and Community: Lessons from Leading Companies, Emerging Economies and a Nine Year Case Study. *Performance Improvement Quarterly, 18.*

——. (2006). *Tecnología del Desempeño Humano.* Chicago: ITSON Business Global Press.

——. (2006). *Desempeño Organizacional.* Chicago: ITSON Business Global Press.

——. (May-June, 2009). Sailing the Winds of "Creative Destruction": Educational Technology During Economic Downturns. *Educational Technology.*

——. (2009). Minding the Business of Business: Tools and Models to Design and Measure Wealth Creation. *Performance Improvement Quarterly, 22* (2) p. 17–72.

Bernardez, M., Kaufman, R., Krivatsy, A., and Arias, C. (in press). City Doctors: A Systemic Approach to Transform Colon City, Panama. *Performance Improvement Quarterly, 24* (4), 41–69.

Bititci, U.S., Turner, T., and Begemann, C. (2000). Dynamics of Performance Measurement Systems. *International Journal of Operations and Production Management, 20* (6), 692–704.

Blenkinsop, S.A. (1993). *Organizational Aspects of Information Processing Systems.* Doctoral Thesis, University of Loughborough.

Brethower, Dale. Personal communication.

Clark, R.E., and Estes, F. (2000). A Proposal for the Collaborative Development of Authentic Performance Technology. *Performance Improvement Quarterly, 39* (4), 48–53.

——. (2002). *Turning Research Into Results: A Guide to Selecting the Right Performance Solutions.* Atlanta, GA: CEP Press.

Cooperrider, D.L., and Srivastva, S. (1987). Appreciative Inquiry in Organizational Life. Research in *Organizational Change and Development, 1,* 129–169.

da Silveira, G., and Slack, N. (2001). Exploring the Trade-off Concept. *International Journal of Operations and Production Management, 21* (7), 949–964.

Davis, I. (2005, May 28). The Biggest Contract. *The Economist*, Vol. 375, No. 8428, p. 87. London.

Dean, P. (1999). Standards on Ethics and Integrity for the Professors and Professionals in the Field of Learning and Performance Improvement and for the Practice of HRD/HPT. *Performance Improvement Quarterly, 12* (3), 3–30.

Deming, W.E. (1972). Code of Professional Conduct. *International Statistical Review, 40* (2), 215–219.

——. (1982). *Quality, Productivity, and Competitive Position.* Center for Advanced Engineering Study. Cambridge, MA: Massachusetts Institute of Technology.

——. (1986). *Out of the Crisis.* Center for Advanced Engineering Technology. Cambridge, MA: Massachusetts Institute of Technology.

——. (1990, May 10). *A System of Profound Knowledge.* Washington, DC: personal memo.

DeVellis, R.F. (2003). *Scale Development: Theory and Applications.* Thousand Oaks, CA: SAGE.

Dick, W., Carey, L., and Carey, J. (2011). *The Systematic Design of Instruction* (7th edition). Boston: Allyn & Bacon.

Eccles, R.G., and Pyburn, P.J. (1992). Creating a Comprehensive System to Measure Performance. *Management Accounting*, 41–44.

Gilbert, T.F. (1978). *Human Competence: Engineering Worthy Performance.* New York: McGraw-Hill.

Grady, M.W. (1991). Performance Measurement, Implementing Strategy. *Management Accounting*, 49–53.

Greenwald, H. (1973). *Decision Therapy.* New York: Peter Wyden, Inc.

Guerra, I. (2001, Jan.). Performance Improvement Based on Results. Is Our Field Interested in Adding Value? *Performance Improvement, 40* (1), 6-10.

——. (2003). Key Competencies Required of Performance Improvement Professionals. *Performance Improvement Quarterly, 16* (1).

——. (2005). How to Develop Useful Questionnaires. *The 2005 Training and Performance Sourcebook*, 233–238.

Guerra-López, I. (2007). *Evaluating Impact: Evaluation and Continual Improvement for Performance Improvement Practitioners.* Amherst, MA: HRD Press, Inc.

———. (2008). Performance Evaluation: Proven Approaches for Improving Program and Organizational Performance. San Francisco: Jossey-Bass.

———. (2010). Performance Tracking and Management Systems. In *Handbook for the Selection and Implementation of Human Performance Interventions*, eds. R. Watkins and D. Leigh. Hoboken, NJ: John Wiley & Sons.

Guerra-López, I., and Norris-Thomas, M. (2011). Making Sound Decisions: A Framework for Judging the Worth of Your Data. *Performance Improvement Quarterly, 50* (5), 37–44.

Guerra-López, I., and Toker, S. (2012). A Performance Measurement and Evaluation Framework for K–12 Environments: Supporting Decision-Making Through Ongoing Performance Measurement. *Evaluation and Program Planning, 35*, 222–235.

Harless, J. (1970). *An Ounce of Analysis Is Worth a Pound of Objectives*. Newman, GA: Harless Performance Guild.

———. (1992). Whither Performance Technology. *Performance & Instruction, 31* (2), 3–8.

International Society for Performance Improvement. (2011). What Is HPT? www.ispi.org (accessed March 31, 2012).

Juran, J.M. (1988). *Juran on Planning for Quality*. New York: The Free Press.

Kaufman, R. (1972). *Educational System Planning*. Englewood Cliffs, NJ: Prentice-Hall. (Also Planificacion de systemas educativos [translation of educational system planning]. Mexico City: Editorial Trillas, S.A., 1973).

———. (1976). *Needs Assessment*. San Diego, CA: University Consortium for Instructional Development and Technology.

———. (1981). Determining and Diagnosing Organizational Needs. *Group and Organizational Studies, 6* (3), 312–322. Amherst, MA: HRD Press, Inc.

———. (1992). *Strategic Planning Plus: An Organizational Guide (Revised)*. Newbury Park, CA: Sage Publishing.

———. (1994, Feb.). Auditing Your Needs Assessment. *T+D* magazine, *48* (2).

———. (1994). Needs Assessment and Analysis. In *Human Resources Management & Development Handbook* (2nd ed.), ed. W.R. Tracey. New York: American Management Association.

——. (1998). *Strategic Thinking: A Guide to Identifying and Solving Problems. Revised.* Washington, DC & Alexandria, VA: The International Society for Performance Improvement and ASTD Press.

——. (2000). *Mega Planning: Practical Tools for Organizational Success.* Thousand Oaks, CA. Sage Publications. Also, *Planificación Mega: Herramientas practicas paral el exito organizacional.* (2004). Traducción de Sonia Agut. Universitat Jaume I, Castelló de la Plana, Espana.

——. (2006). Seven Stupid Things People Do When They Attempt Strategic Thinking and Planning, in *The 2006 ASTD Organization Development & Leadership Sourcebook*, eds. M. Silberman and P. Phillips. Alexandria, VA: ASTD Press.

——. (2006). *Change, Choices, and Consequences: A Guide to Mega Thinking and Planning.* Amherst, MA: HRD Press, Inc.

——. (2009). From Myths to Creating a New Future: A Crisis is a Terrible Thing to Waste. *Performance Improvement, 49* (2), 34–41.

——. (2010, Jan.). Invited Response on the Application of Mega Thinking and Planning to the "Making the Most of Corporate Social Responsibility," *The McKinsey Quarterly.*

——. (2010, Feb.). It's Not the Amount of Money in the Budget. It Is the Measurable Value Added to Florida and Floridians. *Ideas in Action.* Tallahassee, FL, Florida TaxWatch, 1–4.

——. (2010, Mar.–Apr.). Review of *The Management Myth: Why "Experts" Keep Getting it Wrong.* (W.W. Norton, 2009). *Educational Technology*, p. 48–50.

——. (2011). *A Manager's Pocket Guide to Strategic Thinking and Planning.* Amherst, MA: HRD Press, Inc.

——. (2011). Toward a Generic Process for Individual and Organization Performance Improvement and Contribution. P*erformance Improvement, 50*, 32–40.

——. (2012, March). Deriving and Using Vital Signs for Assuring Florida Organizational Viability. *Ideas in Action.* Tallahassee, FL: Florida TaxWatch, 1–8.

Kaufman, R., Corrigan, R.E., and Johnson, D.W. (1969). Towards Educational Responsiveness to Society's Needs: A Tentative Utility Model. *Journal of Socio-Economic Planning Sciences*, 3,151–157.

Kaufman, R., and English, F.W. (1979). *Needs Assessment: Concept and Application.* Englewood Cliffs, NJ: Educational Technology Publications.

Kaufman, R., Stith, M., and Kaufman, J.D. (1992, Feb.). Extending Performance Technology to Improve Strategic Market Planning. *Performance & Instruction Journal, 31* (2), 38–43.

Kaufman, R., Rojas, A.M., and Mayer, H. (1993). *Needs Assessment: A User's Guide.* Englewood Cliffs, NJ: *Educational Technology.*

Kaufman, R., and Clark, R. (1999, Oct.). Re-Establishing Performance Improvement as a Legitimate Area of Inquiry, Activity, and Contribution: Rules of the Road. *Performance Improvement Quarterly, 38* (9), 13–18.

Kaufman, R., and Watkins, R. (2000, Apr.). Getting Serious About Results and Payoffs: We Are What We Say, Do, and Deliver. *Performance Improvement, 39* (4), 23–32.

Kaufman, R., and Bernardez, M. (eds.). (2005). *Performance Improvement Quarterly, 18* (283), special invited issue on mega planning.

Kaufman, R., Guerra, I., and Platt, W.A. (2006). *Practical Evaluation for Educators: Finding What Works and What Doesn't.* Thousand Oaks, CA: Corwin Press/Sage.

Kaufman, R., and Guerra-López, I. (2008). *The Assessment Book: Applied Strategic Thinking and Performance Improvement Through Self-assessments.* Amherst, MA: HRD Press, Inc.

Kaufman, R., Bernardez, M., and Guerra-Lopez, I. (eds.). (2009). *Performance Improvement Quarterly, 22* (2), special invited issue on mega planning.

Lectures in the Performance Improvement Institute Doctoral Program at the Sonora Institute of Technology (Mexico), 2007–2009.

Mager, R. (1997). *Preparing Instructional Objectives: A Critical Tool in the Development of Effective Instruction.* (3rd ed.). Atlanta: Center for Effective Performance.

Mager, R., and Pipe, P. (1970). Analyzing Performance Problems or "You Really Oughta Wanna." Belmont, CA: Fearon.

———. (1999). *Analyzing Performance Problems.* Gastonia, NC: Center for Effective Performance.

Moore, S. (2010). *Ethics by Design: Strategic Thinking and Planning for Exemplary Performance, Responsible Results, and Societal Accountability.* Amherst, MA: HRD Press, Inc.

Moore, S., Ellsworth, J., and Kaufman, R. (2011, July). Visions and Missions: Are They Useful? *Performance Improvement, 50* (6), 15–24.

———. (2008, Aug.). Objectives—Are They Useful? A Quick Assessment. *Performance Improvement, 47* (7) 41–47.

Neely, A.D. (1991). Production Management: A Two-Dimensional Function? *International Journal of Operations and Production Management, 11* (7), 49–54.

———. (1999). The Performance Measurement Revolution: Why Now and What Next? *International Journal of Operations and Production Management, 19* (2), 205–228.

Patton, M.Q. (1997). *Utilization-Focused Evaluation: The New Century Text,* (3rd edition). Thousand Oaks, CA: SAGE.

Pershing, J. (ed.). (2006). *Handbook of Human Performance Technology: Principles, Practices, Potential.* San Francisco: John Wiley & Sons.

Phillips, J.J. (1997). *Return on Investment in Training and Performance Improvement Programs.* Woburn, MA: Butterworth-Heinemann.

Rea, L.M., and Parker, R.A. (1997). *Designing and Conducting Survey Research: A Comprehensive Guide* (2nd edition). San Francisco: Jossey-Bass Publishers.

Richey, R.C. (ed.) (2012). *Encyclopedia of Terminology for Educational and Communications and Technology.* New York: Springer.

Robinson, D., and Robinson, J. (1995). *Performance Consulting: Moving Beyond Training.* San Francisco: Berrett-Koehler Publishers.

Rossett, A. (1987). *Training Needs Assessment.* Englewood Cliffs, NJ: Educational Technology.

Rothwell, W.J. (1996). *Beyond Training and Development: State-of-the-Art Strategies for Enhancing Human Performance.* New York: AMACOM.

Rummerler, G.A., and Brache, A.P. (1995). *Improving Performance: How to Manage the White Space on the Organization Chart* (2nd edition). San Francisco: Jossey-Bass.

Rummler, G.A. (1999). General Systems Theory and Behavioral Psychology. In *Handbook of Human Performance Technology* (2nd edition), eds. H.D. Stolovitch and E.J. Keeps. San Francisco: Pfeiffer.

Rummler, G.A. (2004). *Serious Performance Consulting: According to Rummler.* Silver Spring, MD: International Society for Performance Improvement and the American Society for Training & Development.

Santos, S., Belton, V., and Howick, S. (2002). Adding Value to Performance Measurement by Using System Dynamics and Multicriteria Analysis. *International Journal of Operations and Production Management, 22* (11), 1246–1272.

Scriven, M. (1967). The Methodology of Evaluation. In *Perspectives on Curriculum Evalution*, eds. R. Tyler, R. Gagne, and M. Scriven. New York: McGraw-Hill.

Scriven, M. (1991). *Evaluation Thesaurus* (4th edition). Newbury Park, CA: SAGE.

Skinner, B.F. (1974). *About Behaviorism*. New York: Knopf.

Stevens, S.S. (1951). Mathematics, Measurement, and Psychophysics. In *Handbook of Experimental Psychology*, ed. S.S. Stevens. New York: John Wiley & Sons.

Stolovitch, H.D., Keeps, E.J., and Rodrigue, D. (1999). Skill Sets for the Human Performance Technolgoists. In *Handbook for Human Performance Technology* (2nd edition), eds. H.D. Stolovitch and E.J. Keeps. San Francisco: Pfeiffer.

Stolovitch, H.D. (2000). Human Performance Technology: Research and Theory Into Practice. *Performance Improvement Quarterly, 39* (4), 5–16.

Stufflebeam, D.L., and Webster, W.J. (1980). An Analysis of Alternative Approaches to Evaluation. *Educational Evaluation and Policy Analysis, 2* (3), 5–19.

Suwignjo, P., Bititci, U.S., and Carrie, A.S. (2000). Quantitative Models for Performance Measurement System. *International Journal of Production Economics, 64*, 231–241.

Trinner, D., Greenberry, A., and Watkins, R. (1996). Training Needs Assessment: A Contradiction in Terms? *Education Technology, 36* (3), 51–55.

Watkins, R., and Guerra, I. (2003). Assessing or Evaluating: Determining Which Approach Is Required. In *The 2003 Team and Organizational Development Sourcebook*, eds. M. Siberman and P. Phillips.

Wedman, J., and Graham, S. (1998). The Performance Pyramid. *The Journal of Continuing Higher Education, 46* (3), 8–20.

Westgaard, O. (1988). *A Credo for Performance Technologists*. Western Springs, IL: International Board of Standards for Training, Performance, and Instruction.

Zemke, R. and Kramlinger, T. (1982). *Figuring Things Out: A Trainer's Guide to Needs and Task Analysis*. New York: Basic Books.

GLOSSARY OF TERMS

The increasing responsibilities of professionals for the results, consequences, and payoffs of their activities have led us into a new era of professionalism. For the performance professional this era requires a renewed focus on the scientific-evidence basis for decisions. A basis for this is a consistency in language that leaves no confusion regarding the value added for individuals, organization, and society.

Most of our performance improvement approaches and methods, including the language we use in describing our profession, commonly leave questions concerning value added unanswered. We tend to talk about means (such as HRD, lean Six Sigma, HPT, online training programs), and not ends (such as reduction in poverty, client value added, legitimate profits, product quality). Our language seems almost to encourage a number of confusions that "allows" for lack of precision and consequences. Language that is crisp, to the point, and focused on results (including societal payoffs) is essential for professional success. And then we must match our promises with deeds and payoffs that measurably add value.

What we must communicate to ourselves and others is that the words and phrases are important since they operationally define our profession and communicate our objectives and processes to others. They are symbols and signs with meaning. When our words lead us away, by implication or convention, from designing and delivering useful results for both internal and external clients, then we must consider changing our perspectives and our definitions.

The following definitions come from our review of the literature and other writings. Italics provide some rationale for a possible perspective shift from conventional and comfortable to societal value added. (These are in alphabetical order. At first, some of the definitions won't "follow" but please scan the list for words not yet defined.) In addition, each definition identifies if the word or phrase relates most to a system approach, systems approach, systematic approach, or systemic approach (or a combination). You should begin by reviewing these distinct definitions first, to help you understand the context of these other terms. The level of approach provides the unit of analysis for the words and terms as they are defined in this article. Alternative definitions should also be considered based on the unit of analysis. If we are going to apply system thinking (decision making that focuses on valued added at the individual, organizational, and societal levels) then definitions from that perspective should be applied in our literature, presentations, workshops, and products.

This glossary provides a basis for defining and achieving success in the future through the definitions of terms that focus on the results and payoffs for internal and external clients instead of the process, activities, and interventions we commonly apply.

We've also included cross references to page numbers so the glossary can also serve as an index, directing you to other points in the text where you find each term.

ADDIE Model: A contraction of the conventional instructional systems steps of Analysis, Design, Development, Implementation, and Evaluation. *It ignores or assumes a front determination through assessment of what to analyze, and it also assumes that the evaluation data will be used for continuous improvement.* (3-4, 90)

AADDIE Model: Model proposed by Ingrid Guerra-López that adds Assessment as the first step of the ADDIE Model. (3-4)

Analysis: Breaking something down to its constituent component parts. *Analysis does not formally require that what is being analyzed is useful or correct.* (3-4, 8-9, 24, 46, 57-58, 70-71, 75, 86-97, 103, 111-114, 119, 122-125, 133-137)

Change Creation: The proactive definition and justification of new and evidence-based destinations, and routes are distinguished from change management that is reactive. If this is done before change management, acceptance is more likely. *This is a proactive orientation for change and differs from the more usual "change management" in that it identifies in advance where individuals and organizations are headed rather than waiting for change to occur and be "managed."* (125)

Change Management: Ensuring that whatever change is selected will be accepted and implemented successfully by people in the organization. *Change Management is reactive in that it waits until change requirements are either defined or imposed and then moves to have the change accepted and used.* (86, 98, 125)

Competence: The demonstrated ability to consistently perform at or beyond criteria. (46, 62, 65-66, 74)

Continual/Continuous Improvement: The ongoing check of results with intentions so that changes may be made during an intervention or program. (2-4, 21, 85, 98, 101, 119, 126-127, 156)

Comfort Zones: The psychological areas, in business or in life, where one feels secure and safe (regardless of the reality of that feeling).

Costs-Consequences Analysis: The process of estimating a return-on-investment before an intervention is implemented. It asks two basic questions simultaneously: What do you expect to give and what do you expect to get back in terms of results? *Most formulations do not compute costs and consequences for society and external client (Mega) return-on-investment. Thus, even the calculations for standard approaches steer away from the vital consideration of self-sufficiency, health, and well-being.* (46, 85, 87, 89)

Criteria: Precise and rigorous specifications that allow one to prove what has been or has to be accomplished. Many processes in place today do not use rigorous indicators for expected performance. If criteria are "loose" or unclear, there is no realistic basis for evaluation and continuous improvement. Loose criteria often meets the comfort test but doesn't allow for the humanistic approach to care enough about others to define, with stakeholders, where you are headed and how to tell when you have or have not arrived. (2, 4, 8, 11, 41-43, 46-47, 55-58, 66, 69, 73, 76-77, 79-84, 86-87 95-96, 103, 111-113, 118-119, 133)

Deep Change: Change that extends from Mega—societal value added—downward into the organization to define and shape Macro, Micro, Processes, and Inputs. It is termed "deep change" to note that it is not superficial or just cosmetic, or even a splintered quick fix. *Most planning models do not include Mega results in the change process, and thus miss the opportunity to find out what impact their contributions and results have on external clients and society. The other approaches might be termed "superficial change" or "limited change" in that they only focus on an organization or a small part of an organization.*

Desired Results: Ends (or results) identified through needs assessments that are derived from soft data relating to "perceived needs." *"Desired" indicates these are perceptual and personal in nature.* (5-7, 9-10, 21, 102, 110, 126)

Ends: Results, achievements, consequences, payoffs, and/or impacts. The more precise the results the more likely that reasonable methods and means can be considered, implemented, and evaluated. Without rigor for results statements, confusion can take the place of successful performance. *There are three levels of ends: individual contributions (Micro/Products), Organizational Contributions (Macro/Outputs) and Societal Contributions (Mega/Outcomes). Success requires the linking and aligning of all three levels of results.* (1-2, 4-8, 13-14, 73, 84, 103, 125,132)

Ethics: Know the right and socially responsible thing to do and doing it.

Evidence-Based Practice: The using of research and/or operational performance data that demonstrates the relationship between interventions and consequences.

Evaluation: In its summative version, it compares current status (what is) with intended status (what was intended) and is most commonly done only after an intervention is implemented. For-mative evaluation continuously compares What Is to What Should Be in terms of ends and means throughout development, implementation, and maintenance of an intervention in order to improve it. *Unfortunately, "evaluation" is used for blaming and not fixing or improving. When blame fol-lows evaluation, people tend to avoid the means and criteria for evaluation or leave them so loose that any result can be explained away.* (1-4, 8-11, 15, 62, 78-82, 85-86, 96-99, 101-118, 121,126)

External Needs Assessment: Determining and prioritizing gaps, then selecting problems to be resolved at the Mega level. This level of needs assessment is most often missing from conventional approaches. Without the data from it, one cannot be assured that there will be strategic alignment from internal results to external value added. (23, 28, 49, 61, 73)

Gap Analysis: *This term is commonly, and erroneously, used interchangeably with needs assessment. We suggest needs assessment identifies gaps between current and desired results, while analysis is used to better understand the nature or root causes of the gap.* (55,133)

Hard Data: Performance data that is based on objectives and is independently verifiable. *This type of data is critical. It should be used along with "soft" or perception data.* (10, 38, 54, 105, 112, 114-115)

Human Performance Technology (HPT): An approach that analyzes performance problems, identifies causes of the problems, identifies and develops effective and efficient ways and means to resolve the problems, and then evaluates the results. *Because this approach usually starts with analysis it might assume that the problems of opportunities identified are valid. (See the AADDIE approach). We suggest that the process should begin with needs assessment as the first step, and conclude with actionable recommendations for improvement, after evaluation.* (173)

Human Resource Development (HRD): The actions within an organization to improve the contributions the individuals can and should make to deliver useful results. (111)

Ideal Vision: The measurable definition of the kind of world we, together with others, commit to help deliver for tomorrow's child. *An Ideal Vision defines the Mega level of planning. It allows an organization and all of its partners to define where they are headed and how to tell when they* are getting there or getting closer. It provides the rationality and reasons for an organizational mission objective. (20-21, 27, 29-43, 55, 88-89, 109, 144, 148, 150-152)

Incentives: The rewards and consequences, both tangible and perceptual, that are provided to motivate useful performance. (91-92, 127)

Inputs: The ingredients, raw materials, and physical and human resources that an organization can use in its processes in order to deliver useful ends. *These ingredients and resources are often the only considerations made during planning, without determining the value they add internally and external to the organization.* (14-19, 23, 27-29, 49-50, 61, 73, 75)

Internal Needs Assessment: Determining and prioritizing gaps, then selecting problems to be resolved at the Micro and Macro levels. *Most conventional and popular needs assessment processes are of this variety .* (23, 28, 49, 61, 73)

Lean Six Sigma: A managerial concept intended to result in the elimination or reduction of seven kinds of waste including defects, overproduction, transportation, waiting, inventory, motion, and over-processing. Measurement usually involves reducing variability of what is produced. (173)

Learning: The demonstrated acquisition of a skill, knowledge, attitude, and/or ability not attributed to growth or maturation.

Learning Organization: An organization that sets measurable performance standards and constantly compares its results and their consequences with what is required. Learning organizations use performance data, related to an Ideal Vision and the primary Mission Objective, to decide what to change and what to continue, learning from performance and the organization's contributions. Learning organizations may obtain the highest level of success by strategic thinking: focusing everything that is used, done, produced, and delivered on Mega results—societal value added. *Many conventional definitions do not link the "learning" to societal value added. If there is no external societal linking, than it could well guide one away from the new requirements.*

Macro-Level Planning: Planning focused on the organization itself as the primary client and beneficiary of what is planned and delivered. *This is the conventional starting and stopping place for existing planning approaches.* (x, 14-24, 28-30, 44-47, 49-59)

Means (systems approach, systematic approach): Processes, activities, resources, methods, or techniques used to deliver a result. Means are only useful to the extent that they deliver useful results at all three levels of planned results: Mega, Macro, and Micro. (1, 3-8, 13-14, 55-57, 73-75, 83-84, 103-104, 108, 110)

Mega-Level Planning: Planning focused on external clients, including customers/citizens and the community and society that the organization serves. *This is the usual missing planning level in most formulations. It is the only one that will focus on societal value added: survival, self-sufficiency, and quality of life of all partners. It is suggested that this type of planning is imperative for getting and proving useful results.* Mega planning consists of five steps, or elements for defining and delivering a preferred future that include: 1) deriving the tactical and operational plans; 2) making, buying, and obtaining resources; 3) implementation, and simultaneously, 4) continual improvement/formative evaluation; and then 5) determine effectiveness and efficiency. While not strictly planning, this is the part that puts all of the previous planning to work to achieve positive results. (x, 14-25, 27-48)

Mega Thinking: Thinking about every situation, problem, or opportunity in terms of what you use, do, produce, and deliver as having to add value to external clients and society. Same as strategic thinking.

Methods-Means Analysis: Identifies possible tactics and tools for meeting the needs identified in a "system analysis." The methods-means analysis identifies the possible ways and means to meet the needs and achieve the detailed objectives that are identified in this Mega plan, but does not select them. *Interestingly, this is a comfortable place where some operational planning starts. Thus, it either assumes or ignores the requirement to measurably add value within and outside the organization.* (37, 46, 86-87, 95-97)

Micro-Level Planning: Planning focused on individuals or small groups (such as desired and required competencies of associates or supplier competencies). Planning for building-block results. *This also is a comfortable place where some operational planning starts. Starting here usually assumes or ignores the requirement to measurably add value to the entire organization as well as to outside the organization.* (x, 14-25, 61-72)

Mission Objective: An exact, performance-based statement of an organization's overall intended results that it can and should deliver to external clients and society. *A mission objective is measurable on an interval or ratio scale so states not only "where are we headed" but also adds "how we will know when we have arrived." A mission objective is best linked to Mega levels of planning and the Ideal Vision to ensure societal value added.* (30, 40, 43-46, 52-53, 88)

Mission Statement: An organization's Macro-level "general purpose." A mission statement is only measurable on a nominal or ordinal scale of measurement and only states "where are we headed" and leaves off rigorous criteria for determining how one measures successful accomplishment.

Need: The gap between current results and desired or required results. *This is where a lot of planning "goes off the rails." By defining any gap as a "need" one fails to distinguish between means and ends and thus confuses what and how. If "need" is defined as a gap in results then there is a triple bonus: 1) it states the objectives (What Should Be), 2) it contains the evaluation and continual improvement criteria (What Should Be), and 3) it provides the basis for justifying any proposal by using both ends of a need—What Is and What Should Be in terms of results— proof can be given for the costs to meet the need as well as the costs to ignore the need.* (5-7)

Needs Analysis: Taking the determined gaps between current and desired results and finding the causes of the inability for delivering required results. A needs analysis provides input for the identification of possible ways and means to close the gaps in results—needs—but does not select them. *Unfortunately, "needs analysis" is usually used interchangeably with "needs assessment." They are not the same. How does one "analyze" something (such as a need) before they know what should be analyzed? First assess the needs, then analyze them.* (9)

Needs Assessment: A formal process that identifies and documents gaps between current and desired and/or required results, arranges them in order of priority on basis of the cost to meet the need as compared to the cost of ignoring it, and selects problems to be resolved. *By starting with a needs assessment, justifiable performance data and the gaps between What Is and What Should Be will provide the realistic and rational reason for both what to change as well as what to continue.* (1-3, 7-11)

Objectives: Precise statement of purpose, or destination of where are we headed and how will we be able to tell when we have arrived; the four parts to an objective are 1) what result is to be demonstrated, 2) who or what will demonstrate the result, 3) where the result will be observed, and 4) what interval or ratio scale criteria will be used. *Loose or process-oriented objectives will confuse everyone.* (2, 6-10, 23, 33, 43-46, 49, 52-53, 57, 64-71, 77, 87-90, 98, 101-104, 108-111, 119, 122, 124)

Outcomes: Results and payoffs at the external client and societal level. *Outcomes are results that add value to society, community, and external clients of the organization. These are results at the Mega level of planning.* (15-16, 20, 23, 27-29, 33, 49, 61, 73, 105)

Outputs: The results and payoffs that an organization can or does deliver outside of itself to external clients and society. *These are results at the Macro level of planning where the primary client and beneficiary is the organization itself. It does not formally link to Outcomes and societal well-being unless it is derived from Outcomes and the Ideal (Mega) Vision.* (15-16, 23, 27-29, 49-50, 61, 73, 105)

Paradigm: The framework and ground rules individuals use to filter reality and understand the world around them. *It is vital that people have common paradigms that guide them. That is one of the functions of the Mega level of planning and Outcomes so that everyone is headed to a common destination and may uniquely contribute to that journey.* (33, 141)

Performance: An end, a result, or consequence of any intervention or activity, including individual, team, or organization. (ix-xi, 1-4, 8-11)

Performance Improvement: An attempt to reduce or eliminate the gaps between current results and desired results. *This may be applied to individuals, organizations, or to society/communities.* (87, 90-91, 98, 102-103, 113, 117, 122, 127, 135)

Processes: The means, processes, activities, procedures, interventions, programs, and initiatives an organization can or does use in order to deliver useful ends. *While most planners start here, it is dangerous not to derive the Processes and Inputs from what an organization must deliver and the payoffs for external clients.* (5, 14-19, 23, 27-29, 49-50, 61, 73)

Products: The building-block results and payoffs of individuals and small groups that form the basis of what an organization produces, delivers inside as well as outside of itself, and the payoffs for external clients and society. *Products are results at the Micro level of planning.* (15-16, 18, 23, 27-29, 49-50, 61, 73)

Quasi Need: A gap in a method, resource, or process. *Many so-called "need assessments" are really Quasi needs assessments since they tend to pay immediate attention to means (such as training) before defining and justifying the ends and consequences.* (x, 23, 28, 49, 61, 73-84)

Required Results: Ends identified through needs assessment which are derived from hard data relating to objective performance measures. (8)

Results: Ends, Products, Outputs, Outcomes; accomplishments and consequences. *Usually misses the Outputs and Outcomes.* (ix-x, 1-11, 14-16, 18-21)

Soft Data: Personal perceptions of results. Soft data is not independently verifiable. *While people's perceptions are reality for them, they are not to be relied on without relating to hard—independently verifiable—data as well.* (10, 38, 114-115)

Strategic/Front-End Alignment: The linking of Mega/Outcomes, Macro/Outputs, and Micro/Product level planning and results with each other and with Processes and Inputs. *By formally deriving what the organization uses, does, produces, and delivers to Mega/external payoffs, strategic alignment is complete.* (ix, 2, 27)

Strategic Planning: A proactive approach to planning that starts by identifying gaps between current and desired societal results, putting these needs in priority order, selecting the needs to be reduced and providing the measurable criteria for closing those gaps. *Strategic planning starts with measurably defining Mega.* (13, 15, 24, 30, 33, 40, 43)

Strategic Thinking: Approaching any problem, program, project, activity, or effort with noting that everything that is used, done, produced, and delivered must add value for external clients and society. *Strategic thinking starts with a commitment to Mega.* (24, 30)

System, Systems, Systematic, and Systemic: These terms are related, but not the same. Starting on the systems level and not the system level will mean that we might not add value to external clients and society.

> **System Approach:** Begins with the sum total of parts working independently and together to achieve a useful set of results at the societal level. . .adding value for all internal and external partners. We best think of it as the whole. (32)

> **Systems Approach:** Begins with the parts of a system—subsystems—that make up the "system." So, when someone says they are using a "systems approach" they are really focusing on one or more subsystems. They are unfortunately focusing on the parts and not the whole. When planning and doing at this level, they can only assume that the payoffs and consequences will add up to something useful to society and external clients and this is usually a very big assumption.

> **Systematic Approach:** An approach that does things in an orderly, predictable, and controlled manner. It is a reproducible process. Doing things, however, in a systematic manner does not assure the achievement of useful results. (24)

> **Systemic Approach:** An approach that affects everything in the system. The definition of "the system" is usually left up to the practitioner and may or may not include external clients and society. It does not necessarily mean that when something is systemic it is also useful.

Tactical Planning: Finding out what is available to get from What Is to What Should Be at the organizational/Macro level. Tactics are best identified after the overall mission has been selected based on its linkages and contributions to external client and societal (Ideal Vision) results and consequences. (15, 24, 51)

Wants: Preferred methods and means assumed to be capable of meeting needs. (7-8)

What Is: Current operational results and consequences; these could be for an individual, an organization, and/or society. (4, 8-10, 16, 23, 28, 30, 35, 38-41, 49, 54-55, 58, 61, 67-68, 73, 79-80, 85, 131-137)

What Should Be: Desired or required operational results and consequences; these could be for an individual, an organization, and/or society. (4, 8-10, 16, 23, 28, 30, 35, 38-41, 49, 54-55, 58, 61, 67-68, 73, 79-80, 85, 131-137)

Wishes: Desires concerning means and interventions. It is important not to confuse "wishes" with needs.

What can we surmise by a close consideration of the above definitions and the consideration of the possible perspective (unit of analysis) differences between conventional use and what is suggested here? Here are some:

- System approach ≠ systems approach ≠ systematic approach ≠ systemic approach.
- Mega level planning ≠ Macro level planning ≠ Micro level planning.
- System analysis ≠ systems analysis.
- Means ≠ ends.
- Outcome ≠ Output ≠ Product ≠ Process ≠ Input,
- There are three levels of planning: Mega, Macro, and Micro and three related types of results: Outcomes, Outputs, Products.
- Need is a gap in results, not a gap in Process or Input.
- Needs assessment ≠ needs analysis (nor front-end analysis, or problem analysis).
- Strategic planning ≠ tactical planning ≠ operational planning.
- Change creation ≠ change management.

About the Authors

Roger Kaufman, PhD, is professor emeritus, Florida State University and distinguished research professor at the Sonora Institute of Technology (Mexico). His PhD is in communications from New York University. He consults with public and private organizations in the United States, Mexico, Canada, Australia, New Zealand, Central America, Latin America, and Europe. Kaufman is a Certified Performance Technologist and a Diplomate in School Psychology, a Fellow in Educational Psychology of the American Psychological Association, as well as a Fellow of the American Educational Research Associate. He is the recipient of a U.S. Homeland Security/U.S. Coast Guard medal for Meritorious Public Service. He has been awarded the International Society for Performance Improvement's (ISPI) top two honors: Honorary Member for Life and the Thomas F. Gilbert Award. He is a past ISPI president and a founding member, and is the recipient of ASTD's Distinguished Contribution to Workplace Learning and Performance recognition. Kaufman has published 41 books and more than 280 articles on strategic planning, performance improvement, quality management and continual improvement, needs assessment, management, and evaluation. His latest book is *The Manager's Pocket Guide to Mega Thinking and Planning.* You may reach him by email at: rkaufman@nettally.com.

Ingrid Guerra-López, PhD, is an associate professor and director of the Institute for Learning and Performance Improvement at Wayne State University and currently serves on the board of directors of the International Society for Performance Improvement (ISPI). Guerra-López's research, teaching, and consulting focus on improving human and organizational performance through needs assessment and evaluation, with particular focus on performance monitoring and evaluation systems. Her book, *Performance Evaluation: Proven Approaches for Improving Program and Organizational Performance*, is one of the most widely used evaluation books in instructional systems and performance improvement graduate programs at universities. She has published six books on assessment and evaluation, more than 40 articles in highly respected peer reviewed journals, and over a dozen book chapters on performance improvement, assessment, and evaluation in seminal books. Guerra-López has worked internationally with government, community service organizations, education, military, and corporate clients. She has also coached leaders all over the world, across 28 different countries, with primary focus in Latin America, working with clients in Mexico, Venezuela, Colombia, Argentina, Chile, and Brazil, El Salvador, Costa Rica, Mexico, Panama, Venezuela, Colombia, Argentina, and Brazil. Her most recent project includes assessments and performance improvement projects for various ministries in Africa.

HOW TO PURCHASE ASTD PRESS PRODUCTS

All ASTD Press titles may be purchased through ASTD's online store at **www.store.astd.org**.

ASTD Press products are available worldwide through various outlets and booksellers. In the United States and Canada, individuals may also purchase titles (print or eBook) from:

Amazon– www.amazon.com (USA); www.amazon.com (CA)
Google Play– play.google.com/store
EBSCO– www.ebscohost.com/ebooks/home

Outside the United States, English-language ASTD Press titles may be purchased through distributors (divided geographically).

**United Kingdom, Continental Europe,
the Middle East, North Africa, Central Asia,
and Latin America:**
Eurospan Group
Phone: 44.1767.604.972
Fax: 44.1767.601.640
Email: eurospan@turpin-distribution.com
Web: www.eurospanbookstore.com
For a complete list of countries serviced via Eurospan please visit www.store.astd.org or email publications@astd.org.

South Africa:
Knowledge Resources
Phone: +27(11)880-8540
Fax: +27(11)880-8700/9829
Email: mail@knowres.co.za
Web: http://www.kr.co.za
For a complete list of countries serviced via Knowledge Resources please visit www.store.astd.org or email publications@astd.org.

Nigeria:
Paradise Bookshops
Phone: 08033075133
Email: paradisebookshops@gmail.com
Website: www.paradisebookshops.com

Asia:
Cengage Learning Asia Pte. Ltd.
Email: asia.info@cengage.com
Web: www.cengageasia.com
For a complete list of countries serviced via Cengage Learning please visit www.store.astd.org or email publications@astd.org.

India:
Cengage India Pvt. Ltd.
Phone: 011 43644 1111
Fax: 011 4364 1100
Email: asia.infoindia@cengage.com

For all other countries, customers may send their publication orders directly to ASTD. Please visit: **www.store.astd.org**.